Species Under Threat

Editor: Tina Brand

me 332

1776563

Independence Educational Publishers

First published by Independence Educational Publishers

The Studio, High Green

Great Shelford

Cambridge CB22 5EG

England

© Independence 2018

ISBN-13: 978 1 86168 783 8

Printed in Great Britain

Zenith Print Group

Contents

Introduction

SPECIES UNDER THREAT is Volume 332 in the **ISSUES** series. The aim of the series is to offer current, diverse information about important issues in our world, from a UK perspective.

ABOUT SPECIES UNDER THREAT

A "biological annihilation" of wildlife in recent decades means a sixth mass extinction in Earth's history is under way. Tens of thousands of species – including 25 per cent of all mammals and 13 per cent of birds – are now threatened with extinction because of over-hunting, poaching, pollution, loss of habitat, the arrival of invasive species, and other human-caused problems. This book explores the reasons why and looks at the relationship between humans and the rest of the natural world. It also explores what is being done to protect the species which are currently under threat.

OUR SOURCES

Titles in the **ISSUES** series are designed to function as educational resource books, providing a balanced overview of a specific subject.

The information in our books is comprised of facts, articles and opinions from many different sources, including:

⇨ Newspaper reports and opinion pieces

⇨ Website factsheets

⇨ Magazine and journal articles

⇨ Statistics and surveys

⇨ Government reports

⇨ Literature from special interest groups.

A NOTE ON CRITICAL EVALUATION

Because the information reprinted here is from a number of different sources, readers should bear in mind the origin of the text and whether the source is likely to have a particular bias when presenting information (or when conducting their research). It is hoped that, as you read about the many aspects of the issues explored in this book, you will critically evaluate the information presented.

It is important that you decide whether you are being presented with facts or opinions. Does the writer give a biased or unbiased report? If an opinion is being expressed, do you agree with the writer? Is there potential bias to the 'facts' or statistics behind an article?

ASSIGNMENTS

In the back of this book, you will find a selection of assignments designed to help you engage with the articles you have been reading and to explore your own

Useful weblinks

www.animalaid.org.uk

www.bristol.ac.uk

www.buglife.org.uk

www.theconversation.com

www.ed.ac.uk

www.huffingtonpost.co.uk

www.ibtimes.co.uk

www.independent.co.uk

www.inews.co.uk

www.panda.org

www.ptes.org

www.qmul.ac.uk

www.rarebirdalert.co.uk

www.royalholloway.ac.uk

www.telegraph.co.uk

www.theguardian.com

www.uea.ac.uk

www.wildlifetrusts.org

opinions. Some tasks will take longer than others and there is a mixture of design, writing and research-based activities that you can complete alone or in a group.

FURTHER RESEARCH

At the end of each article we have listed its source and a website that you can visit if you would like to conduct your own research. Please remember to critically evaluate any sources that you consult and consider whether the information you are viewing is accurate and unbiased.

Rainforest collapse in prehistoric times changed the course of evolution

An article from **The Conversation.**

THE CONVERSATION

By Emma Dunne, PhD student, University of Birmingham

Over 750,000 square kilometres of Amazon rainforest have been cleared since 1970 – a fifth of the total. As a result, many of the animals that live there are threatened with extinction. But this isn't the first time the Earth has seen its rainforests shrink. Toward the end of the Carboniferous period, around 307 million years ago, the planet's environment shifted dramatically, and its vast tropical rainforests vanished.

Palaeontologists have previously struggled to work out how this rainforest collapse affected the first ancient vertebrate animals that lived there – the early tetrapods. This is because the fossil record for this time is patchy and incomplete. My colleagues and I have now published new research that reveals how the collapse initially caused the number of species to fall, affecting water-loving amphibians the most. But this event ultimately paved

the way for the ancestors of modern reptiles, mammals and birds – known as the amniotes – to flourish and spread across the globe.

About 310 million years ago, long before the first dinosaurs and mammals evolved, North America and Europe lay in a single landmass at the equator covered by dense tropical rainforests, known as the 'coal forests'. The warm, humid climate and rich vegetation provided an ideal habitat for amphibian-like early tetrapods. This allowed them to quickly diversify into a variety of species.

Toward the end of the Carboniferous period, the number of tetrapod species had begun to increase greatly. But then the climate became much drier, causing a mass extinction of many species in the dominant plant groups, such as horsetails and club mosses.

Although the collapse of the rainforests

was a catastrophic event for plants, how it affected early tetrapods has remained largely uncertain. Previous analyses suggest that the number of early tetrapod species increased through the collapse of the rainforests, but that the resulting fragmented landscape isolated different groups from each other, a pattern known as endemism.

Fossil bias

The problem with this research is that the early tetrapod fossil record is heavily biased. Much of what we know about early tetrapod evolution comes from extensively-studied fossil sites in midwestern and southern US, western Canada and central Europe. This means our picture of early tetrapod evolution is biased around how much effort has been put into finding and identifying fossils from these areas.

As with the dinosaurs, the reptile-like tetrapods of the Permian period, such as the sail-backed Dimetrodon, have captivated palaeontologists for many years. In contrast, the animals and landscapes of the Carboniferous period are relatively understudied. Palaeontologists and geologists are collaborating to close these gaps in our knowledge. Together, these biases limit our knowledge of early tetrapod diversity and can drastically affect analyses.

To address this problem, my colleagues and I turned to the Paleobiology

Database. This database is accessible to the public and is updated continuously by palaeobiologists with the location and age of all fossil finds from across the world. Instead of simply counting the species we have fossils for, we applied innovative statistical methods to the entire tetrapod fossil record.

Our results, published in the *Proceedings of the Royal Society B*, reveal that tetrapod species diversity decreased after the rainforest collapse, with amphibians suffering the greatest losses. The drier climate would have reduced the amount of suitable habitats for amphibian species, which are dependent on wet environments and must return to water to spawn.

Instead of evidence for endemism, we found that tetrapod species that survived the rainforest collapse began to disperse more freely across the globe, colonising new habitats further from the equator. Many of these survivors were early amniotes, such as diadectids and synapsids, animals that had considerable advantages over amphibians. They were generally larger so could travel longer distances, and because they laid eggs they were not confined to watery habitats.

While the fossil record of the Carboniferous and early Permian periods is strongly biased, new statistical methods that address these biases have allowed us to examine the true impact of the rainforest collapse on early tetrapods. We now know that the event was crucial in paving the way for amniotes, the group that ultimately gave rise to the dinosaurs and eventually modern reptiles, mammals and birds, to become the dominant group of land vertebrates.

7 February 2018

⇨ The above information is reprinted with kind permission from *The Conversation*. Please visit www. theconversation.com for further information.

Earth's sixth mass extinction event under way, scientists warn

Researchers talk of "biological annihilation" as study reveals billions of populations of animals have been lost in recent decades.

By Damian Carrington, Environment Editor

A "biological annihilation" of wildlife in recent decades means a sixth mass extinction in Earth's history is under way and is more severe than previously feared, according to research.

Scientists analysed both common and rare species and found billions of regional or local populations have been lost. They blame human overpopulation and overconsumption for the crisis and warn that it threatens the survival of human civilisation, with just a short window of time in which to act.

The study, eschews the normally sober tone of scientific papers and calls the massive loss of wildlife a "biological annihilation" that represents a "frightening assault on the foundations of human civilisation".

Professor Gerardo Ceballos, at the Universidad Nacional Autónoma de México, who led the work, said: "The situation has become so bad it would not be ethical not to use strong language."

Previous studies have shown species are becoming extinct at a significantly faster rate than for millions of years before, but even so extinctions remain relatively rare giving the impression of a gradual loss of biodiversity. The new work instead takes a broader view, assessing many common species which are losing populations all over the world as their ranges shrink, but remain present elsewhere.

The scientists found that a third of the thousands of species losing populations are not currently considered endangered and that up to 50% of all individual animals have

been lost in recent decades. Detailed data is available for land mammals, and almost half of these have lost 80% of their range in the last century. The scientists found billions of populations of mammals, birds, reptiles and amphibians have been lost all over the planet, leading them to say a sixth mass extinction has already progressed further than was thought.

The scientists conclude: "The resulting biological annihilation obviously will have serious ecological, economic and social consequences. Humanity will eventually pay a very high price for the decimation of the only assemblage of life that we know of in the universe."

They say, while action to halt the decline remains possible, the prospects do not look good: "All signs point to ever more powerful assaults on biodiversity in the next two decades, painting a dismal picture of the future of life, including human life."

Wildlife is dying out due to habitat destruction, overhunting, toxic pollution, invasion by alien species and climate change. But the ultimate cause of all of these factors is "human overpopulation and continued population growth, and overconsumption, especially by the rich", say the scientists, who include Professor Paul Ehrlich, at Stanford University in the US, whose 1968 book *The Population Bomb* is a seminal, if controversial, work.

"The serious warning in our paper needs to be heeded because civilisation depends utterly on the plants, animals and microorganisms of Earth that supply it with essential ecosystem services ranging from crop pollination and protection to

Nearly half of the mammal species surveyed lost more than 80% of their distribution between 1900 and 2015

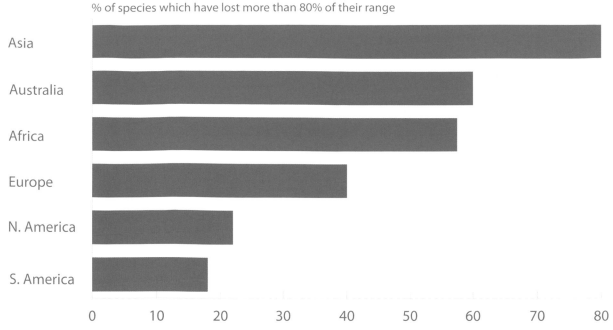

% of species which have lost more than 80% of their range

supplying food from the sea and maintaining a livable climate," Ehrlich told *The Guardian*. Other ecosystem services include clean air and water.

"The time to act is very short," he said. "It will, sadly, take a long time to humanely begin the population shrinkage required if civilisation is to long survive, but much could be done on the consumption front and with 'band aids' – wildlife reserves, diversity protection laws – in the meantime." Ceballos said an international institution was needed to fund global wildlife conservation.

The research analysed data on 27,500 species of land vertebrates from the IUCN and found the ranges of a third have shrunk in recent decades. Many of these are common species and Ceballos gave an example from close to home: "We used to have swallows nesting every year in my home near Mexico City – but for the last ten years there are none."

The researchers also point to the "emblematic" case of the lion: "The lion was historically distributed over most of Africa, southern Europe and the Middle East, all the way to northwestern India. [Now] the vast majority of lion populations are gone."

Professor Stuart Pimm, at Duke University in the US and not involved in the new work, said the overall conclusion is correct, but he disagrees that a sixth mass extinction is already under way: "It is something that hasn't happened yet – we are on the edge of it."

Pimm also said there were important caveats that result from the broad-brush approach used. "Should we be concerned about the loss of species across large areas – absolutely – but this is a fairly crude way of showing that," he said. "There are parts of the world where there are massive losses, but equally there are parts of the world where there is remarkable progress. It is pretty harsh on countries like South Africa which is doing a good job of protecting lions."

Robin Freeman, at the Zoological Society of London, UK, said: "While looking at things on aggregate is interesting, the real interesting nitty gritty comes in the details. What are the drivers that cause the declines in particular areas?"

Freeman was part of the team that produced a 2014 analysis of 3,000 species that indicated that 50% of individual animals have been lost since 1970, which tallies with the new work but was based on different IUCN data. He agreed strong language is needed: "We need people to be aware of the catastrophic declines we are seeing. I do think there is a place for that within the [new] paper, although it's a fine line to draw."

Citing human overpopulation as the root cause of environmental problems has long been controversial, and Ehrlich's 1968 statement that hundreds of millions of people would die of starvation in the 1970s did not come to pass, partly due to new high-yielding crops that Ehrlich himself had noted as possible.

Ehrlich has acknowledged "flaws" in *The Population Bomb* but said it had been successful in its central aim – alerting people to global environmental issues and the role of human population in them. His message remains blunt today: "Show me a scientist who claims there is no population problem and I'll show you an idiot."

10 July 2017

⇨ The above information is reprinted with kind permission from *The Guardian*. Please visit www.theguardian.com for further information.

Humans are ushering in the sixth mass extinction of life on Earth, scientists warn

"Extinction rates for birds, mammals and amphibians are similar to the five global mass-extinction events of the past 500 million years that probably resulted from meteorite impacts, massive volcanism and other cataclysmic forces."

By Ian Johnston, Environment Correspondent

Humans are bringing about the sixth mass extinction of life on Earth, according to scientists writing in a special edition of the leading journal *Nature*.

Mammals, birds and amphibians are currently becoming extinct at rates comparable to the previous five mass extinctions when "cataclysmic forces" – such as massive meteorite strikes and supervolcano explosions – wiped out vast swathes of life, including the dinosaurs.

The growing human population – which has increased by 130 per cent in the last 50 years and is set to rise to more than ten billion by 2060 – and our increasing demand for resources as we become wealthier is ramping up the pressure on the natural world.

Tens of thousands of species – including 25 per cent of all mammals and 13 per cent of birds – are now threatened with extinction because of over-hunting, poaching, pollution, loss of habitat, the arrival of invasive species, and other human-caused problems.

But the researchers said it was not "inevitable" that this process would continue. There is still time for humans to turn the situation around by protecting habitats, changing our diets to less land-intensive food, and taking other forms of conservation.

In one of a series of papers in *Nature*, a team of international scientists wrote: "The ever-increasing and unprecedented extent and impact of human activities on land and in the oceans over the past few centuries has dramatically reduced global biodiversity.

"There is overwhelming evidence that habitat loss and fragmentation, over-exploitation of biological resources, pollution, species invasions and climate change have increased rates of global species extinctions to levels that are much higher than those observed in the fossil record."

And we are not immune from such problems.

This loss of biodiversity could "substantially diminish the benefits that people derive from nature", they warned.

In order to preserve such "ecosystem services", policies should be designed to "secure the valuable and often irreplaceable benefits of biodiversity for future generations, even under conditions of rapid global change", the paper added.

Another paper painted a bleak picture of humans' long history of wiping out other animals.

"Human-influenced extinctions began when modern humans moved out of Africa," it said.

"Successive waves of extinctions in Australia (50,000 years ago), North America and South America (10,000–11,000 years ago) and Europe (3,000–12,000 years ago) were driven largely by a combination of hunting by humans and natural climate change.

"By 3,000 years ago, Earth had lost half of all terrestrial mammalian megafauna species (with a mass of more than 44kg) and 15 per cent of all bird species."

The researchers said that since 1500AD, human destruction of wildlife had "accelerated".

"Extinction rates for birds, mammals and amphibians are similar at present to those of the five global mass-extinction events of the past 500 million years that probably resulted from meteorite impacts, massive volcanism and other cataclysmic forces," they wrote.

It said "urgent" action was needed to ensure that "sufficient habitats will remain to preserve the viability of. . . species in the long term and to guarantee that such habitats are well managed".

"All species could benefit from the intensification of current conservation policies, as well as from policies that reduce underlying anthropogenic threats," the paper added.

"Developing and enacting such policies, however, will require an unprecedented degree of engagement between stakeholders, policymakers, natural scientists and social scientists.

"Earth is capable of providing healthy diets for ten billion people in 2060 and preserving viable habitats for the vast majority of its remaining species.

"The benefits for biodiversity and humanity of pursuing these goals are great, and with forethought and timely action, these goals can be achieved."

31 May 2017

⇨ The above information is reprinted with kind permission from *The Independent*. Please visit www.independent.co.uk for further information.

© *independent.co.uk 2018*

Climate change is making rare breeding birds increasingly vulnerable to extinction, new RSPB report warns

"Birds in the UK are showing changes in abundance and distribution."

By Kathryn Snowdon

Rare breeding birds are becoming increasingly vulnerable to extinction in the UK due to climate change, a new report reveals.

Species such as dotterel, whimbrel, common scoter and Slavonian grebe are all said to be in danger, based on projections around the impact of global warming.

The findings come from a new report compiled by the RSPB, the British Trust for Ornithology (BTO) and the Wildfowl and Wetlands Trust (WWT), along with various statutory nature conservation bodies.

Experts fear that the Scottish crossbill, which is found only in Scotland, is at risk of becoming extinct altogether.

By contrast, however, some other birds were found to have thrived in the warmer, wetter climate, which has enabled them to expand their range further north.

The study found climate change is already affecting bird life in the four countries of the UK, which is responding to a 1° C (1.8° F) increase in average summer temperatures since the 1980s.

"Birds in the UK are showing changes in abundance and distribution, predominantly moving northwards, in a way that is consistent with a changing climate," the report said.

"Migratory birds are arriving earlier and egg-laying dates have advanced such that swallows, for example, are arriving in the UK 15 days earlier, and breeding 11 days earlier, than they did in the 1960s."

For species such as the dotterel, whimbrel, common scoter and snow bunting – whose UK breeding populations are found almost entirely in Scotland – population declines are said to have been considerable already.

Breeding success of the Slavonian grebe has also been impacted, with Scotland on average 11% wetter between 2007–2016 than it was in 1961–1990.

The report went on: "The UK's kittiwake population has declined by 70% since 1986 because of falling breeding success and adult survival.

"Climate change has reduced the availability of the sandeels they rely upon in the breeding season.

"Other species that feed largely on sandeels, such as Arctic skua, Arctic tern and puffin, are at high risk of climate-related decline."

On a more positive note, the report also found that warmer temperatures during the breeding season have had a positive effect on breeding success for a range of species.

Birds that feed insects to their young, such as great tits and chaffinches, have improved their productivity in warm, dry springs, while nuthatch, goldfinch and chiffchaff have been expanding their range into Scotland over the last 30 years with large increases in numbers north of the border.

Dr David Douglas, principal conservation scientist at RSPB Scotland, said: "The recent research compiled in this year's *The State of the UK's Birds* report shows that many birds in Scotland are being affected by a changing climate.

"For some birds this means they are becoming increasingly vulnerable to UK extinction, including many species where most, if not all, of the breeding population is found in Scotland.

"Other birds appear to have thrived in this warmer, wetter climate, which has

allowed them to expand their range further north."

Colette Hall, of WWT, said: "Each winter, tens of thousands of waterbirds migrate to the UK and our long-running network of volunteer waterbird counters has tracked their changes over decades.

"Warmer winters on the continent have meant more birds of certain species wintering further east, such as the European white-fronted goose.

"However, that trend can mask real declines in some species, such as the Bewick's swan and the common pochard.

"For this reason, amongst many others, it is vital we continue to monitor our bird populations so we can pinpoint where, and subsequently try to work out why, these changes are happening."

5 December 2017

⇨ The above information is reprinted with kind permission from The Huffington Post UK. Please visit www.huffingtonpost.co.uk for further information.

Threats to oceans and coasts

Oceans. For centuries people have regarded them as an inexhaustible supply of food, a useful transport route, and a convenient dumping ground – simply too vast to be affected by anything we do. But human activity, particularly over the last few decades, has finally pushed oceans to their limit.

Major threats to the world's oceans include:

UNSUSTAINABLE FISHING

90% of the world's fisheries are already fully exploited or overfished, while billions of unwanted fish and other animals die needlessly each year. Unsustainable fishing is the largest threat to ocean life and habitats . . . not to mention the livelihoods and food security of over a billion people.

INADEQUATE PROTECTION

They might cover over 70% of our planet's surface, but only a tiny fraction of the oceans has been protected: just 3.4%. Even worse, the vast majority of the world's few marine parks and reserves are protected in name only. Without more and better managed Marine Protected Areas, the future of the ocean's rich biodiversity – and the local economies it supports – remains uncertain.

TOURISM & DEVELOPMENT

The beach is not just a favourite holiday destination, it's our favourite place to live. Around the world, coastlines have been steadily turned into new housing and tourist developments, and many beaches all but disappear under flocks of holiday-makers each year. This intense human presence is taking its toll on marine life.

SHIPPING

The oceans are huge highways, across which we ship all kinds of goods. Like other human activities, this heavy traffic is leaving its mark: oil spills, ship groundings, anchor damage, and the dumping of rubbish, ballast water and oily waste are endangering marine habitats around the world.

OIL & GAS

Important reserves of oil, gas and minerals lie deep beneath the seafloor. However, prospecting and drilling for these poses a major threat to sensitive marine habitats and species.

POLLUTION

Untreated sewage, garbage, fertilisers, pesticides, industrial chemicals, plastics . . . most of the pollutants on land eventually make their way into the ocean, either deliberately dumped there or entering from water run-off and the atmosphere. Not surprisingly, this pollution is harming the entire marine food chain – all the way up to humans.

AQUACULTURE

Fish farming is often touted as the answer to declining wild fish stocks. But more often than not, the farming of fish and shellfish is actually harming wild fish, through the pollution the farms discharge, escaped farmed fish, increased parasite loads and the need to catch wild fish as feed.

CLIMATE CHANGE

Coral bleaching, rising sea levels, changing species distributions – global warming and climate change are already having a marked affect on the oceans. Strategies are needed to deal with these phenomena, and to reduce other pressures on marine habitats already stressed by rising water temperatures and levels.

2017

⇨ The above information is reprinted with kind permission from the World Wildlife Fund International. Please visit www.panda.org for further information.

From five billion to zero: the passenger pigeon – and other beautiful animals driven to extinction

By Oliver Smith, Digital Travel Editor

Here are ten iconic species no longer on Earth, largely thanks to humans.

1. Passenger pigeon

A nomadic bird that could reach speeds in excess of 60mph, the passenger pigeon was once across North America, from the Great Plains to the Atlantic Coast. At the height of their population they numbered up to five billion, making them the most populous species of bird on the planet.

That was until the arrival of Europeans, who hunted them on an industrial scale for cheap meat. Tens of millions were slaughtered each year and the last wild passenger pigeon was seen in 1901. Cincinnati Zoo was home to the last captive bird, Martha, which died exactly 103 years ago (1 September, 1914).

"Passenger Pigeons once migrated through Canada, the United States and the Gulf of Mexico in numbers so huge that they darkened the sky," says the website of the American Natural History Museum. "One flock was described as 'a column, eight or ten miles in length... resembling the windings of a vast and majestic river'. In 1808, one flock of passenger pigeons in Kentucky was estimated at more than two billion birds. Today, they are extinct owing to a combination of results of human activity, including the destruction of their food sources, westward expansion and overhunting."

Where it roamed: North America, to the east of the Rockies.

Closest living relative: They are closely related to *Patagioenas*, a genus of New World pigeons, of which there are 17 species.

2. Dodo

Perhaps the most famous extinct species, the dodo – endemic to Mauritius – was wiped out in just a few decades. The first recorded mention of the flightless bird was by Dutch sailors in 1598; the last sighting of one in 1662. It owes much of its fame to its appearance in *Alice's Adventures in Wonderland*.

On its website the Natural History Museum says: "Despite the abundance of the dodo on Mauritius during the 17th century, very little remains in museums as evidence of its existence. There are a few partial skeletons of the bird; a skull in Copenhagen, a beak in Prague, a foot at the Natural History Museum and a head and foot in Oxford. The one known complete stuffed bird was in the collection of John Tradescant who bequeathed it to the Ashmolean Museum in Oxford. Here, the specimen was allowed to rot, so that by 1755 the directors of the Museum consigned it to the bonfire. It is thanks to the dedication of one curator from the Ashmolean Museum that the head and foot were saved and these are now in the Oxford University Museum of Natural History."

Where it roamed: Mauritius.

Closest living relative: The Nicobar pigeon, found in the Andaman and Nicobar Islands, India.

3. Western black rhinoceros

This subspecies of the black rhino once roamed sub-Saharan Africa, but fell victim to poaching. Its population was in the hundreds in 1980, fell to ten by 2000, and just five a year later. Surveys in 2006 failed to locate any and it was declared extinct in 2011.

Where it roamed: The last survivors were found in Cameroon.

Closest living relative: The black rhinoceros, native to eastern and southern Africa, which is critically endangered.

4. Pyrenean ibex

Extinct since 2000, the Pyrenean ibex – a subspecies of the Spanish ibex – was once common to the Pyrenees but its population fell sharply in the 19th and 20th centuries. The reasons behind its decline remain unknown. In 2003 it briefly became "unextinct", after a scientist managed to clone a female, but it died minutes after being born.

Where it roamed: The Pyrenees.

Closest living relative: Two of the four subspecies of the Spanish ibex still exist: the Western Spanish ibex, found in the Picos de Europa, and the Southeastern Spanish ibex, common in the Sierra Nevada.

5. Quagga

A subspecies of plains zebra, with stripes only on the front half of its body, the quagga lived in South Africa. It was heavily hunted after Dutch settlers arrived and found it competing with domesticated animals for forage. It was extinct in the wild by 1878; the last captive specimen died in Amsterdam in 1883.

Where it roamed: South Africa.

Closest living relative: Burchell's zebra, which thrive in Namibia's Etosha National Park.

6. Tasmanian tiger

A shy, nocturnal animal and similar in appearance to a dog (but with a stiff tail and abdominal pouch), the Tasmanian tiger was rare or extinct on the Australian mainland before the arrival of the British, but survived on Tasmania. Hunting, disease, the introduction of dogs and human encroachment all contributed to its demise there. The last known specimen died in Hobart Zoo in 1936.

"Known as the Tasmanian wolf, Tasmanian tiger, zebra dog, pouched wolf and marsupial dog, among others," says the website of the American Museum of Natural History. "A quick look at the animal explains the confusion. Shaped like a dog, striped like a tiger or zebra, pouched like an opossum, and reputed to behave like a wolf, it became many different creatures in the popular imagination."

Where it roamed: Tasmania.

Closest living relative: Tasmanian devil, still found on the island, but endangered.

7. Steller's sea cow

The largest mammals, other than whales, to have existed in the holocene epoch, the Steller's sea cow reached up to nine metres in length but was hunted to extinction in 1768, within 27 years of its discovery by Europeans.

Georg Wilhelm Steller described its hide as "more like unto the bark of an ancient oak than unto the skin of an animal" and "almost impervious to an axe or the point of a hook". Its blunt forelimbs were also of particular interest. "There are no traces of fingers, nor are there any of nails or hoofs," he wrote. "With these he swims, as with branchial fins; with these he walks on the shallows of the shore, as with feet; with these he braces and supports himself on slippery rocks; with these he digs out and tears off the algae and seagrasses from the rocks, as a horse would do with its front feet; with these he fights." A complete skeleton can be seen in Helsinki's Natural History Museum.

Where it roamed: Its last population surrounded the uninhabited Commander Islands, part of the Aleutian Islands in the northern Pacific.

Closest living relative: The dugong, found in coastal areas of the Indian and south-west Pacific oceans, and the manatee (also known as sea cows), found in the Caribbean (West Indian manatee), West Africa (West African manatee), and the Amazon (Amazonian manatee). All are considered vulnerable.

8. Woolly mammoth

The woolly mammoth, which reached heights in excess of three metres and weighed up to six tonnes, coexisted with early humans, who used its bones and tusks for making tools and dwellings and also hunted it for food. Small populations survived on St Paul Island, off the coast of Alaska, and Wrangel Island, in the Arctic Ocean, until 5,600 and 4,000 years ago, respectively.

Where it roamed: Arctic regions of Asia and North America.

Closest living relative: The Asian elephant, itself considered endangered.

9. Great auk

Once common to the North Atlantic, including the coast of Britain, the great auk – like penguins, though unrelated – was flightless, clumsy on land, but an agile swimmer. Demand for its down contributed to its elimination from Europe, while early explorers used it as a convenient food source. It has been extinct since at least 1852.

London's Natural History Museum houses a specimen from the island of Papa Westray. It says: "The flightless great auk, *Pinguinus impennis*, is one of the most powerful symbols of the damage humans can cause. The species was driven extinct in the 19th century as a consequence of centuries of intense human exploitation."

Where it roamed: The North Atlantic.

Closest living relative: The razorbill, found in the North Atlantic, including Iceland.

10. Pinta Island tortoise

This subspecies of Galápagos tortoise is widely considered extinct, with the last known specimen – Lonesome George – dying in 2012. A recent trip by Yale University researchers, however, suggested that Isabela Island, the largest of the Galápagos, could still be home to the species.

Where it roamed: Pinta Islands, The Galápagos.

Closest living relative: Giant tortoises can still be seen on seven islands in the Galápagos, and the Aldabra atoll, in the Indian Ocean.

1 September 2017

⇨ The above information is reprinted with kind permission from *The Telegraph*. Please visit www.telegraph.co.uk for further information.

Hydroelectric dams threaten Brazil's mysterious Pantanal – one of the world's great wetlands

THE CONVERSATION

An article from **The Conversation.**

By Lauren Crabb, Lecturer in Organisational Behaviour and Human Resources, Coventry University; Anna Laing, Lecturer in International Development, University of Sussex; Bronwen Whitney, Senior Lecturer in Physical Geography, Northumbria University, Newcastle and Carlos Saito, Professor of Geography, Northumbria University, Newcastle

The Pantanal in central South America may not be as globally famous as the Amazon rainforest, but it has the continent's highest concentration of wildlife. Now, however, the region's endangered plants and animals, along with its still undiscovered secrets, may be wiped out in return for cheap hydroelectricity.

The Pantanal is the world's largest tropical wetland and covers an area slightly larger than England. It lies mostly on a huge floodplain at the foot of Brazil's southwestern highlands, but a fraction also spills over into Bolivia and Paraguay. In the wet season, from October to April, water washes down from those highlands bringing with it nutrients and fish and leaving most of the region underwater. When the rains finish, and the ground dries up, the landscape changes once again.

Seasonal variation on such a massive scale means the Pantanal contains a diverse range of plants and animals that have adapted to thrive in standing water or waterlogged soil. The region is home to more than 1,000 bird species and 300 mammals including the jaguar, capybara, giant otter and tapir.

Yet the Pantanal is now threatened by Brazil's thirst for hydroelectricity. We are part of a group of researchers investigating the state of Mato Grosso, where the rush to build dams is particularly apparent. Mato Grosso holds the upper reaches of the Pantanal, but is probably more famous for the Amazon rainforest in the north of the state and the enormous 'fazendas' (large farms) on its fringes which produce soya, beef and cotton.

This mixture of natural resources and fertile land means Mato Grosso has a long history of environmental issues. However, if the state today is recognised as a deforestation hotspot, soon it may be known for its dams. This is because the height difference between the rainy plateau in the north of the state and its southern plains means there is lots of hydroelectric potential.

Mato Grosso is following a nationwide trend. After a series of major blackouts in 2001 which highlighted Brazil's energy insecurities, the country turned to hydroelectricity. Since then, a wave of dams have been, or are planned to be, constructed to satisfy the ever increasing demand for energy.

Over the past few years, Brazil's growth acceleration programme has allowed for the increased construction of hydroelectric dams in the state, while also removing or weakening some environmental laws.

There are already 38 operational hydroelectric plants in the Paraguay river's upper basin, the region that drains into the Pantanal. A further 94 are due to be built in coming years.

In Brazil, dams are classified in two categories: those that are able to produce more than 30MW of energy, and small hydroelectric plants (SHP) with a capacity of less than 30MW and a reservoir of less than 13km^2. These small plants are seen as more environmentally friendly and are commonly constructed as part of a chain along the length of the river.

In the Amazon, the impacts of the bigger dams have been well documented. Fish numbers are down, and irregular floods have exposed dry land that had previously been submerged during the wet season.

Less research has been conducted in the Pantanal basin but the few reports that have investigated dams there report similar results. Additionally, one larger dam led to river depth fluctuating by several metres over weekly or even daily periods, confusing fish and affecting water quality. Less is currently known about the impacts of the smaller hydroelectric dams but, as they still store some water in the reservoir in order to produce energy at peak times, especially in low-flow rivers, they thus also affect the river's daily fluctuations.

What we do know is that too many dams on the rivers that feed the Pantanal would disrupt the natural rhythm of the wetland. Large-scale cattle ranchers, soy farmers and city dwellers drive year-round demand for water and energy, which would put the seasonal flood 'pulse' at risk. In this scenario, species that have adapted themselves over thousands of years to life in an on-off wetland may find themselves thrown out of sync.

Even several small plants close to each other can produce new patches of still surface water, fragmenting ecosystems and affecting ecological relationships. Meanwhile, those whose livelihoods are dependent on these cycles, mainly traditional fishing communities, may find they can no longer survive.

As the impacts of hydroelectric dams become apparent in the Amazon, it is crucial that we do not forget the Pantanal. If the wetland is going to survive, it will take a concerted effort from all actors who use its resources to work together. The Pantanal is a complex ecosystem where society and the environment clash on a number of issues. With the increasing demand for electricity and solar and wind options being little investigated in Mato Grosso, it is important the full impacts of hydroelectric generation are known.

6 November 2017

⇨ The above information is reprinted with kind permission from *The Conversation*. Please visit www. theconversation.com for further information.

Turtle doves "nearing UK extinction because of farming practices"

By Victoria Ward

Turtle doves are on the brink of extinction in the UK because of farming practices, it has been claimed.

Numbers have plummeted by 70 per cent in five years, leading the RSPB to call for an urgent "overhaul" of the current agricultural system as the UK leaves the EU and its system of subsidies, to support wildlife and farming.

Latest statistics from the Environment Department (Defra) revealed that birds living and breeding on the UK's farmland saw numbers tumble by almost a tenth between 2010 and 2015.

Their populations have declined by 56 per cent since 1970, largely due to agricultural changes including the loss of mixed farming, a switch to autumn sowing of crops, a reduction in hay meadows and the stripping out of hedgerows.

Corn buntings, grey partridge and tree sparrows are among the species which have suffered "severe" declines of more than 90 per cent since 1970.

Capercaillie and willow tit have also seen a similarly concerning reduction in numbers over the same period.

But while the majority of the decline happened between the late 1970s and 1980s as farming practices changed rapidly, there was a nine per cent decline between 2010 and 2015.

The data showed some "specialist" species, those restricted to or highly dependent on farmland habitats, had seen precipitous falls.

But the fall was most dramatic for turtle doves, a traditional symbol of love and fidelity, with numbers down 71 per cent between 2010 and 2015.

The decline in UK numbers of the birds, which migrate from wintering grounds in Africa to breed in Europe, is mirrored across the continent and conservationists have warned the turtle dove is at risk of going extinct globally.

The sharp drop in numbers is thought to be down to a lack of seeds from arable plants which has shortened their breeding season and led to fewer nesting attempts. The RSPB's head of land use policy, Jenna Hegarty, said: "Birdsong from some of our most iconic species once filled the air, but for many years the soundtrack of our countryside – from the song of the skylark to the purr of the turtle dove – has become quieter and quieter.

"Today's figures show the number of farmland birds continues to drop. The farmland bird indicator has fallen by nine per cent in the last five years – the worst period of decline since the late 1980s.

"Many farmers are doing great things, and without their efforts, today's figures would undoubtedly be worse.

"But the current agriculture system doesn't work for our farmers or our natural environment, something needs to change.

"Leaving the EU gives us a seminal opportunity to overhaul the system, and use public money to build a more sustainable future, reversing the

dramatic declines in farmland wildlife and supporting resilient and thriving farm businesses into the future."

Elsewhere in the countryside, woodland birds have seen numbers remain relatively stable over the last five years, although they are down almost a quarter since 1970.

Across all species, including farmland, woodland, wetland and waterbirds and seabirds, numbers are down around eight per cent on 1970, the figures show.

Some species, such as stock doves and goldfinches, saw populations double.

23 November 2017

⇨ The above information is reprinted with kind permission from *The Telegraph*. Please visit www.telegraph.co.uk for further information.

China's demand for rare $50,000 "aquatic cocaine" fish bladder pushing species to extinction

Rare organ now one of the most sought-after aphrodisiacs in the world.

By Lucy Pasha-Robinson

China's illegal trade in the rare totoaba fish's swim bladder is driving both it and the endangered vaquita, the world's smallest porpoise, to the brink of extinction, according to a new report.

Numbers of the vaquita have been decimated by illegal poachers using gill nets to trap the totoaba fish, nicknamed "money maw" or "aquatic cocaine" for its staggeringly high price tag on the Asian market.

While prices have fallen in recent years, some large totoaba bladders can still fetch more than $50,000 each on the Chinese black market.

Both species are found only in the northernmost corner of Mexico's Cortez Sea and both are critically endangered, with only 60 vaquita thought to be left in the wild.

The totoaba fish are highly sought after for their alleged health benefits in treating circulatory and skin problems and are believed by some to hold aphrodisiac properties.

The Environmental Investigations Agency (EIA) are now warning of a "buoyant trade" in China, with "no attempt to curb the practice" despite repeated condemnation from environmental activists.

EIA oceans campaign head Clare Perry said the Chinese Government needed to acknowledge its vital role in saving the endangered vaquita species.

"Trade is happening openly of the totoaba in mainland China despite it being illegal, and we actually found a whole new centre for the trade in Shantou that had clearly seen no efforts from the Chinese Government," she told The Independent.

"Given the information out there, it's quite a shocking lack of law enforcement when you have the survival of a species at risk."

Ms Perry also warned of a lack of incentive for Mexican smugglers to stop the poaching, warning it was a low-risk alternative to cocaine smuggling, with high reward.

She said: "The trade has been going on for over a century.

"However, when Mexican fisherman started making a lot of money, the organised crime groups got involved, as they do with all of these wildlife products where they see quick profit.

"That's when the trade really exploded."

Julian Newman, EIA's campaigns director said dual responsibility needed to be taken to effectively stamp out the trade between the Mexican suppliers of the maw and the Chinese market driving the fishing.

In 2015, Mexican federal environment agency Profepa revealed the commodity was worth more than cocaine in the country, with one kilo of bladder selling for the same as 1.5 kilos of the drug.

In an attempt to stamp out the practice, the Mexican military scours the 5,019-square-mile stretch of Californian Gulf several times a day looking for poachers.

Speaking to Mexican newspaper Reforma, one army chief, who wished to remain anonymous, said: "Traffickers entered the business forcefully, applying their organisational structures and their corrupting influence.

"Organised crime has established networks, routes, contacts, points of sale and padrinos, or sponsors, in official institutions.

"What was once used to traffic drugs was implemented for the totoaba."

However, the Mexican Secretariat of Environment and Natural Resources (Semarnat) reported that traffickers often camouflaged the bladders with other legally-fished maw.

One environment official said: "The training of police agents isn't enough, be it at the municipal, state or federal levels.

"The situation is the same with the Army, Navy and customs personnel: they're not trained to detect these crimes."

The vaquita is the smallest and rarest cetacean species, closely resembling the common porpoise.

Ms Perry said it was not clear that China had a full understanding of the implications of the totoaba trade for the vaquita.

She said: "Domestically, China must stamp out the illegal trade, but also some very swift awareness raising needs to happen among business traders and consumers to save this critically endangered species."

20 September 2016

⇨ The above information is reprinted with kind permission from *The Independent*. Please visit www.independent.co.uk for further information.

Trophy hunting may cause extinction in a changing environment

Trophy hunting and other activities involving the targeting of high-quality male animals could lead to the extinction of certain species faced with changing environmental conditions, according to new research from Queen Mary University of London (QMUL).

Male animals with large secondary sexual traits, such as antelope horns, deer antlers and lions' manes are often targeted by hunters for recreational purposes. Similarly, some insect collectors will pay high prices for specimens of animals such as stag beetles because of their large secondary sexual traits.

These well-ornamented individuals tend to be the most evolutionarily fit so if they are removed then the best genes are taken out of the population. The researchers predict that in some circumstances, when an animal population is faced with a changing environment, harvesting rates of as low as five per cent of these high quality males can cause extinction.

The study was published in *Proceedings of the Royal Society B: Biological Sciences*.

Lead author Dr Rob Knell, from QMUL's School of Biological and Chemical Sciences, said: "This demonstration that trophy hunting can potentially push otherwise resilient populations to extinction when the environment changes is concerning. Because these high-quality males with large secondary sexual traits tend to father a high proportion of the offspring, their 'good genes' can spread rapidly, so populations of strongly sexually selected animals can adapt quickly to new environments. Removing these males reverses this effect and could have serious and unintended consequences.

"We found that 'selective harvest' has little effect when the environment is relatively constant, but environmental change is now a dangerous reality across the globe for considerable numbers of species."

A force for conservation

Trophy hunting is an important industry – a greater land area of sub-Saharan Africa is conserved for hunting than is protected in national parks – and it is thought to have little effect on well-managed harvested populations because off-take rates are low and usually only the males are targeted.

Using a computer simulation model, however, the researchers were able to predict the impact of selectively targeting males on the basis of their secondary sexual traits and how the environment affects this.

In addition to the careful reactive management of harvested populations, they suggest removing only older males which have already had an opportunity to reproduce.

Dr Knell said: "Our results clearly show that age restrictions on harvest which allow males to breed before they are taken is effective at reducing the impact of selective harvest on adapting populations.

"When properly regulated, trophy hunting can be a powerful force for conservation which is why we're suggesting a different management approach as opposed to calling for a ban."

Trophy hunters and insect collectors are not the only people targeting males on the basis of their secondary sexual ornaments. Many animal populations harvested for food are managed by only allowing the harvest of males and in at least some of these, such as certain crab populations, males with big secondary sexual traits are targeted.

Furthermore, elephant tusks function partly as secondary sexual traits and poachers will specifically target elephants based on tusk size. This research suggests that these populations might be at more risk than was previously thought.

29 November 2017

⇨ The above information is reprinted with kind permission from Queen Mary University of London. Please visit www.qmul.ac.uk for further information.

© 2018 Queen Mary University of London

Size not important for fish in the largest mass extinction of all time

Understanding modern biodiversity and extinction threats is important. It is commonly assumed that being large contributes to vulnerability during extinction crises.

However, researchers from the University of Bristol and the Chengdu Center of the China Geological Survey, have found that size played no role in the extinction of fish during the largest mass extinction of all time.

The study focused on the evolution of bony fishes during the Permian-Triassic mass extinction 252 million years ago. During this crisis, as many as 90 per cent of all species on Earth were killed by massive climate change triggered by huge volcanic eruptions in Russia.

The erupted gases led to worldwide acid rain and atmospheric warming of as much as 20 degrees centigrade. This killed plants, and soil was stripped by rainfall and washed into the sea. Oceans were also heated and life fled from the tropics.

It was expected that a key feature in extinction would have been body size: the large animals would suffer heat and starvation stress first. However, in the new paper, published today in *Palaeontology*, it is shown that larger fish were no more likely to go extinct than small fish.

The study used a detailed summary of all information on fossil fish through a span of over 100 million years, from well before to well after the disaster. Body size information was identified for over 750 of these fishes, and multiple calculations were carried out to allow for variations in the shape of the evolutionary tree and the exact dating of all the species. The result was clear – body size did not provide any advantages or disadvantages to fish during the crisis.

Lead researcher Dr Mark Puttick from the Natural History Museum and University of Bristol's School of Earth Sciences, explained: "These results continue the trend of recent studies that suggest body size played no role in determining which species survive or go extinct. This is the opposite result we would expect, but provides increasing support for previous studies that show body size plays no role in extinction selectivity."

The team explored the largest dataset used in an analysis of this type and applied a range of computational evolutionary models to understand these patterns in deep time. The models take account of uncertainties in the quality of the fossil data and the reconstructed evolutionary tree, and the result was clear.

Professor Michael Benton, also from the University of Bristol, added: "These are exciting results. What is important also is that we were able to deploy new methods in the study that take greater account of uncertainties.

"The methods are based around a detailed evolutionary tree so, unlike most previous work in the field, we paid attention to the relationships of all the species under consideration."

Professor Shixue Hu, leader of the China Geological Survey: "It's great to see this new analytical work. We were able to include many new fossils from our exceptional biotas in China, and we can see the full impact of the extinction and the subsequent recovery of life during the Triassic."

30 June 2017

⇨ The above information is reprinted with kind permission from the University of Bristol. Please visit www.bristol.ac.uk for further information.

Why are so many animals in danger?

It is estimated that there could be as many as 14 million species of plants and animals in the world, although only around two million have been officially recorded so far. More than 12,000 species of animals and plants now face extinction, due largely to human activities. Some will die out before they have even been discovered.

Habitat destruction

Tropical rainforests are the world's richest natural habitats, housing more than two-thirds of all plant and animal species on earth. Sadly, the rainforests are being destroyed at an alarming rate – with more than half already gone – for timber, and cleared so that the land can be used to graze farmed animals or to provide housing for expanding human populations. If rainforests disappear, all the plants and animals living there will be lost forever.

Six species of great ape who live in the tropical rainforests – the eastern and western gorilla, chimpanzee, bonobo, Sumatran and Bornean orang-utan – now face extinction. This is due to habitat destruction, and hunting.

Pandas live in the bamboo forests of China, another habitat that is being destroyed to make way for a rapidly growing human population. The panda population has been reduced to 1500.

Hunting and trapping

People kill animals for their fur (to make coats and rugs), for their bones and horn (to make medicine or ornaments), for their flesh, and, sometimes, sadly, simply for the fun of it. Many animals are also trapped in the wild to supply the pet trade, or for use in circuses, zoos and aquaria. Others – in particular, primates – are captured and sold to research laboratories to be used in experiments.

The Tiger is just one of many species of wild cat now facing extinction because of hunting and habitat loss.

At the beginning of the 20th century, there were more than 100,000 tigers. Today, it is estimated that between 5,000 and 7,000 tigers remain in the wild. Three of the eight sub-species (the Bali, Caspian and Javanese) are already extinct. In the past, tigers were hunted for their skins (to make coats and rugs) and for sport. Today, tigers are still being killed for traditional Asian medicine. Virtually all of their body parts, including bones, eyes and whiskers, are used. Many Asian countries have recently signed up to the conservation agreement known as CITES and have agreed to ban the trade in tiger parts. Enforcing the law, however, is difficult and costly, while the profits made from the illegal trade are so great that some people feel it is worth the risk.

CITES (the Convention On International Trade in Endangered Species)

CITES is a United Nations agreement that protects endangered species by regulating or banning their trade. Unfortunately, not all countries belong to CITES, and enforcement efforts vary among those that have signed up. Even when someone is prosecuted, the punishments are usually trivial – ranging from minimal fines to short jail sentences, and are therefore little deterrent.

Wildlife trafficking is one of the major forms of smuggling in the world, along with drugs and weapons.

Whales have been ruthlessly hunted for centuries and, as a result, several species – including the giant blue whale – have been driven to the brink of extinction. This prompted the International Whaling Commission (IWC) to impose a moratorium (ban) on all commercial whaling in 1985. Norway, Japan and Iceland have continued to kill some species of whales .

Rhinos have roamed the Earth for more than 40 million years, but after only a few centuries of intensive hunting they are now severely threatened. The world population of all five species is fewer than 15,000 animals.

Rhinos are killed for their horn, which is ground up and used in traditional Asian medicine. This slaughter continues despite a CITES ban on the trade.

African elephants, the world's largest land animals, have also suffered a catastrophic decline. A century ago there were 10 million animals, 20 years ago there were one million, but today there are only about 300,000 African elephants left. Most were killed for their ivory tusks, which are made into trivial trinkets and jewellery. In 1990, CITES banned the sale and trade in ivory and other elephant products but many elephants are still illegally shot by poachers.

Pollution

Rivers, seas and lakes are being poisoned with sewage, oil and toxic chemicals from industry. Human refuse also pollutes the environment and kills wildlife. Crops are sprayed with chemicals to kill bugs and insects, which in turn harm the animals who feed on them. Global warming and climate change caused by, amongst other factors, air pollution,

also threatens lots of species with extinction.

In 2004, researchers identified 146 dead zones around the world's coastlines, areas where the dissolved oxygen levels are so low that no marine life can be sustained.

The animals who live in the oceans, particularly those at the top of the food chain, absorb these poisonous chemicals (including pesticides and industrial waste). For example, the bodies of seals, whales and dolphins and even Arctic polar bears have been found to contain high levels of toxic chemicals, which damage their ability to reproduce.

Why does it matter?

Some people say that we should conserve animals and plants because they might be useful to us in the future. It is also argued that, in the long term, our own survival may depend on maintaining the planet's ecosystems. This means preserving other species and maintaining the planet's biodiversity – or variety of life.

Animal Aid believe quite simply that we have a responsibility to protect animals for their own sake and especially those species which are at risk because of our actions.

Solutions

⇨ Conserve the world's natural habitats. Keeping alive endangered species in zoos is not a solution, because it becomes enormously difficult and expensive to repatriate them to their natural habitat. If we carry on polluting and destroying these habitats, repatriation becomes literally impossible. Only through protection of their habitats will wild animals survive.

⇨ Ban the international trade in products made from endangered species and enforce the laws that already exist to protect wildlife.

⇨ Educate people to help stop the trade in animal products.

⇨ Stop polluting the environment with poisonous wastes.

⇨ The above information is reprinted with kind permission from Animal Aid. Please visit www.animalaid.org.uk for further information.

© 2018 Animal Aid

Most large herbivores now face extinction, our study shows

THE CONVERSATION

An article from The Conversation.

By Matt Howard, Senior Lecturer in Conservation, Bangor University and William Ripple, Distinguished Professor and Director, Trophic Cascades Program, Oregan State University

Until relatively recently, lots of different massive mammals roamed across our planet. Mastodons, mammoths, giant elk, rhinoceros-sized marsupials, sabre-toothed cats, marsupial lions, dire wolves, American cheetahs... the list goes on and on. Then modern humans spread throughout the world and the vast majority of those large species disappeared. Our planet's large mammal biodiversity is a shade of what it once was.

Sadly, research we've carried out shows that the large mammal extinctions of the past 2.5 million years are continuing today – and smaller species are now also threatened.

Our new study, published in *Science Advances*, reviewed the threats, status and ecosystem services provided by the 74 largest terrestrial herbivores (exceeding 100kg in body mass), and the conservation effort required to save them from extinction.

Our results are highly concerning. The vast majority of these large herbivores are declining in distribution and abundance, such that 60% are now threatened with extinction. These include well-known and iconic species such as elephants, hippos, all species of rhino, European bison and Indian water buffalo, but also less well-known species such as takin, kouprey, mountain and lowland anoa, and tamaraw. The situation is likely to get worse and we risk leaving empty landscapes unless urgent and drastic action is undertaken.

Hunting, habitat loss and competition for food with livestock are the major threats to the world's large herbivores. Simply identifying these threats is perhaps the most optimistic result of our study, as these are all issues that can be managed and reduced, provided there is sufficient human will to do so.

Development issue

While Africa supports the greatest number of large herbivore species, south-east Asia retains the most that are threatened. The region's woodlands are facing empty forest syndrome – where they seem intact, but there are few large animals left within them.

Overwhelmingly, it is developing countries that host the remaining megafauna – they are largely gone from the developed world. Consequently, these poorer nations bear the costs of protecting large herbivores, as well as the missed opportunity costs of setting aside large areas of land for conservation rather than food production. The developed world offers paltry support.

Research efforts also suffer from this same disparity. Data deficiency is the bane of conservation management, yet the most-studied large herbivores are the common game species. We know next to nothing about large and highly threatened wild pigs such as Oliver's warty pig or the Palawan bearded pig, for instance. Without adequate and targeted funding, it is hard to see this research occurring before it is too late for many of the developing world's big herbivores.

Life without big beasts

A world without elephants, tapirs, hippos, giraffes or gorillas would be a much poorer place. Large herbivores

are inspirational, and huge numbers of tourists travel the world to observe them.

Yet these species also perform fundamental roles in the ecosystems they inhabit and their loss would substantially alter the natural world. African elephants knock over trees enabling shrubland to develop, for example. This shrubland benefits browsing species such as impalas and black rhinos.

Elephants also make great seed dispersers and there are concerns that this ecosystem service is being lost in parts of Asia and Africa where they are becoming scarce. Other large herbivores have also been shown to have a disproportionate impact on their environment, such that their decline is likely to have repercussions right along the food chain.

The return of bears and wolves to Europe illustrates that developed countries can succeed in conserving wildlife. These large carnivores can also play fundamental roles in their ecosystems, often by limiting numbers of common herbivores such as rabbit or deer, yet globally carnivores are also still in decline.

There are plans to reintroduce beavers, lynx and wild boar in the UK, as wolves have been returned to Yellowstone National Park in the US. But what about the mega-herbivores? Why don't we bring back herds of wild cattle (the ecological equivalent and modern variant of the extinct aurochs) to the UK? Governments are inherently risk averse when it comes to conservation initiatives, but they must start acting before it is too late for these majestic creatures.

1 May 2015

⇨ The above information is reprinted with kind permission from *The Conversation*. Please visit www.theconversation.com for further information.

Puffins and turtle doves at risk of being wiped out, say experts

"Global wave of extinction lapping at UK shores" as latest list of endangered species classifies birds alongside African elephant and lion.

By Caroline Davies

Puffin and turtle dove numbers across the globe have plummeted so rapidly the birds now face the same extinction threat as the African elephant and lion, say conservationists.

Atlantic puffins and European turtle doves have been added for the first time to the International Union for Conservation of Nature (IUCN) red list of species at risk of being wiped out.

In total, four UK bird species have been added to the new list, doubling to eight the number of bird species commonly seen in Britain now given official "vulnerable" status. A further 14 UK species are considered "near threatened".

African vultures fare even worse, with six of the 11 vulture species now deemed "critically endangered" – the highest category of threat before extinction – mainly due to the indiscriminate laying of poisoned bait for leopards, lions or hyenas, deliberate poisoning by poachers, and the use of vulture body parts in traditional medicine, the RSPB said.

Martin Harper, the RSPB's conservation director, said: "Today's announcement means that the global wave of extinction is now lapping at our shores. The number of species facing extinction has always been highest in the tropics, particularly on small islands. But now the crisis is beginning to exact an increasingly heavy toll on temperate regions too, such as Europe.

"The erosion of the UK's wildlife is staggering and this is reinforced when you talk about puffin and turtle dove now facing the same level of extinction threat as African elephant and lion, and being more endangered than the humpback whale," he said.

The crash in Atlantic puffin numbers in Norway, Iceland and the Faroe Islands, which together hold 80% of the European population, has been linked to climate change and fishing practices. In Britain there have been significant losses on Fair Isle and Shetland, though elsewhere in the UK numbers are better.

Though puffin numbers remain in their millions in Europe, there have been worryingly high breeding failures at key colonies. Dr Richard Gregory, the RSPB's head of species monitoring, said: "The red listing is driven by the declines in Europe, where most of the population is, particularly in Iceland and Norway."

The small bird faced a "long list of threats", he said. Research showed puffins were particularly susceptible to shifts in sea temperatures, thermal mixing and extreme weather, all affecting their prey species of sand eels, sprats and other small fish.

Gill net fisheries and invasive predators such as rats, cats and mink on the islands where they breed, as well as fishing of their prey species, have also contributed to the decline, he said.

The turtle dove, once a familiar summer visitor to much of Europe, including south-east England, has suffered declines across the continent of more than 30% over the past 16 years. The decline in the UK has been particularly high, with more than nine out of every ten birds lost since the 1970s.

"We are researching a number of different reasons why, including changes in agricultural practice across Europe, which means a struggle to find food and nesting sites," said Grahame Madge, an RSPB spokesman.

As a migratory bird across two continents, it is vulnerable to being hunted while migrating. "We do know there is strong illegal hunting of turtle dove around the Mediterranean," said Madge. Changes in land-use patterns and climate shifts in sub-Saharan Africa are also deemed to have potentially impacted on the birds.

The Slavonian grebe, mainly found in North America but also in decline in the Scottish Highlands, is evaluated as "vulnerable" in the list, announced on Thursday by BirdLife International on behalf of the IUCN.

UK wading birds added to the "near threatened" category include the knot, curlew, sandpiper, bar-tailed godwit, oystercatcher and lapwing. Among sea ducks, the long-tailed duck and the velvet scoter are listed as "vulnerable", as is the pochard.

The vulture crisis has now spread from Asia to Africa, with the situation described as "incredibly serious". In Asia, vultures have experienced a 99.9% decline as farmers treat livestock with the anti-inflammatory drug diclofenac, which is poisonous to vultures, said Madge.

African vultures had been doing better, but are now suffering from poisons set out for leopards or hyenas by farmers protecting stock. A growing threat is from poachers. "Poachers are putting out poison to try and ensure the vultures don't give away their crime," the RSPB spokesman said.

Vultures are also killed in the belief that ingesting their brains bestows special powers. "So this is very troubling for vultures. We have seen the declines in southern Asia, and now we are seeing this very dramatic decline in their populations in Africa, through persecution, incidental or deliberate," he added.

29 October 2015

⇨ The above information is reprinted with kind permission from *The Guardian*. Please visit www.theguardian.com for further information.

Illegal trade pushing helmeted hornbills towards extinction

Researchers are sounding the alarm for the helmeted hornbill after a new study of seizure figures revealed 2,170 hornbill heads or casques had been confiscated from illegal trade in just three years.

The figures were obtained from enforcement actions in Indonesia and China between March 2012 and August 2014, with Indonesia accounting for over half the parts seized.

Trade in the helmeted hornbill *Rhinoplax vigil*: the 'ivory hornbill' warns that the high numbers of casques in illegal trade point to a significant demand for the keratin-filled structure or casque on the bird's bill, which is carved into luxury decorations and jewellery, akin to elephant ivory.

The hornbills are poached on the islands of Sumatra and Kalimantan in Indonesia and often then shipped to China, where their casques are carved and sold as status symbols, said the report published in *Bird Conservation International*.

The authors also highlighted several other indications of a mounting threat from the trade such as the discovery of helmeted hornbill casques in multiple-species seizures that included tigers, rhinos, elephants and pangolins – other threatened wildlife species highly desired by traffickers.

Investigations by conservation groups in Sumatra and Kalimantan have shown the hornbill trade is being orchestrated by organised criminal gangs, with syndicates commissioning teams of poachers to hunt the birds.

The 2015 IUCN Red List assessment notes the species has apparently almost disappeared from habitats where it was previously abundant on Sumatra and cautions that poaching efforts could shift to Malaysia from Indonesia, where illegal capture is now focused.

"If this problem isn't dealt with very soon, the helmeted hornbill may be wiped out in Indonesia and seriously threatened elsewhere," said Dr Chris R. Shepherd, Regional Director for TRAFFIC in Southeast Asia whose work on the report was funded by Wildlife Reserves Singapore.

"The health of the rainforests will suffer and the forests will fall silent."

Hornbills are essential to rainforest ecosystems as they help with seed dispersal through their droppings. The call of the Helmeted Hornbill is also one of the most charismatic sounds of the region's rainforests.

The study calls for a slew of urgent measures to arrest the problem including greater patrolling and monitoring, far-reaching investigations into the criminal networks controlling the trade and increased vigilance at hotspots in China and Indonesia.

The helmeted hornbill is found in parts of western Indonesia, Malaysia, southern Thailand and the tip of southern Myanmar, in low densities. It is protected by local laws throughout its native range, and is listed in Appendix I of the Convention on International Trade in Endangered Species of Wild Fauna and Flora (CITES), which prohibits its commercial international trade. Hunting continues despite these protections.

In 2015, due to the severe increase in poaching for the illegal trade, the helmeted hornbill was reclassified from Near Threatened to Critically Endangered on the IUCN Red List of Threatened Species.

11 May 2016

⇨ The above information is reprinted with kind permission from Rare Bird Alert. Please visit www.rarebirdalert.co.uk for further information.

Even zoos can no longer protect rhinos from poachers

THE CONVERSATION

An article from **The Conversation.**

By Tanya Wyatt, Associate Professor of Criminology, Northumbria University, Newcastle

Zookeepers at Thiory Zoo, near Paris, recently arrived at work to find their four-year-old rhinoceros, Vince, dead from a gunshot to the head. The larger of his two horns had been cut off with a chainsaw. The poachers responsible had forced open one grille and two locked doors in order to get into the rhino's enclosure. Police presume that the smaller horn was not taken, and the zoo's other two rhinos were not killed, because the poachers either did not have time or were interrupted.

There is speculation that the poachers are 'professionals' and the horn will be smuggled to Asia.

No matter how shocking and heartbreaking it is to hear about the murder of this rhino, it should come as little surprise. In their native habitats the five species of rhino are at best 'near threatened' and at worst 'critically endangered' because they are poached for their horns. According to the charity Save the Rhino the total worldwide population was around 500,000 at the beginning of the 20th century. Today, there are just 29,000 left.

Vince's species, the southern white rhino, is actually a conservation success story, as it has come back from the brink of extinction a century ago to an estimated population of at least 19,000. The good news ends there though. The black rhino population is estimated to be just over 5,000 individuals; the greater one-horn rhino over 3,500, and the Javan and Sumatran rhinos both under 100. Even the southern white's numbers can't protect it from poaching: if current death rates continue, it may become extinct in the wild by 2023.

There are huge profits to be made from poaching rhinos. Demand from Asia, where there is a long history of rhino horn in traditional medicine, means each horn can fetch tens or hundreds of thousands of dollars on the black market. This makes it one of the most expensive commodities in the world – potentially more valuable per kilo than diamonds or cocaine.

But poaching in the wild is getting harder. Anti-poaching technology is getting smarter, wardens are being militarised, and there are simply fewer rhinos left to target. The logical next step is for poachers and organised crime to adapt and choose 'soft' targets such as zoos, safari parks and sanctuaries. There's evidence this is already happening: an Irish organised crime group, the Rathkeale Rovers, is allegedly responsible for 60 rhino horn thefts from natural history museums across Europe.

Poaching in the west may not even be limited to 'organised' crime groups. In the case of Vince the rhino, one grille, two locked doors and some surveillance cameras are not exactly sophisticated technology that 'unorganised' criminals wouldn't be able to get around.

But we shouldn't be surprised if Vince's killers turn out to be professionals. Organised crime, like most wildlife crime, adapts to conditions and looks for new opportunities to make money. Zoos seem to be ready targets where the benefits are very high and the risk of getting caught very low.

The horn is probably on its way to Asia, but let's not forget that Europe is one of the three top consumers of illegal wildlife. China and the US are the other two. So while Europeans may have a reputation for being wildlife and animal lovers, there is a dark side to the continent's relationship with wildlife that is often ignored.

Zoos and safari parks should increase their security measures and vigilance as chances are rhinos will not be the only victims of poaching in Europe because of the illegal wildlife trade. And that's regardless of whether the demand is from inside or outside of Europe and if the poachers are organised crime or not.

9 March 2017

⇨ The above information is reprinted with kind permission from *The Conversation*. Please visit www.theconversation.com for further information.

More than 700 species facing extinction are being hit by climate change

Humans' closest relatives, the primates, are among those worst affected because their tropical habitats have had a stable climate for thousands of years.

By Ian Johnston, Environment Correspondent

More than 700 mammals and birds currently threatened with extinction already appear to have been adversely affected by climate change, according to a major review of scientific studies.

Primates and marsupials are believed to have the most individual species suffering as a result of global warming, according to a paper in the journal *Nature Climate Change*.

Only two groups of mammals, rodents and insect-eaters, are thought to have benefited. This is partly because they have fast breeding rates, tend not to be specialists suited to a particular habitat, and often live in burrows which provide insulation against changes in the weather.

The figures are much higher than previously thought, making up 47 per cent of land mammals and 23 per cent of the birds on the International Union for Conservation of Nature's Red List of species threatened with extinction.

According to the list itself, just seven per cent of the mammals and four per cent of the birds are described as being threatened by "climate change and severe weather".

The researchers developed a model to compare the animals' weight and other characteristics with changes in the climate, such as the temperature.

"Using this model, we estimated that 47 per cent of terrestrial [non-flying] threatened mammals (out of 873 species) and 23.4 per cent of threatened birds (out of 1,272 species) may have already been negatively impacted by climate change in at least part of their distribution," the article in *Nature Climate Change* said.

"Our results suggest that populations of large numbers of threatened species are likely to be already affected by climate change, and that conservation managers, planners and policy makers must take this into account in efforts to safeguard the future of biodiversity."

Primates and marsupials are more at risk than other animals partly because they have lived mostly in tropical parts of the world which have had a stable climate for thousands of years.

"Many of these [animals] have evolved to live within restricted environmental tolerances and are likely to be most affected by rapid changes and extreme events," the paper added.

"In addition, primates and elephants are characterised by very slow reproductive rates that reduce their ability to adapt to rapid changes in environmental conditions."

One reason why climate change is causing a problem for animals is changes in the distribution of plants.

"In areas with reduced precipitation and/or temperature seasonality, it is likely that plant species may have narrower climatic tolerances, and therefore that these areas may have already experienced vegetation changes with consequential loss of habitat for animals living there," the paper said.

"A more specialised diet was also associated with greater probability of negative responses in mammals.

"Our findings are in agreement with previous studies on the predictors of general extinction risk, in which species with narrower diet breadths were associated with lower ability to exploit resources and adapt to new environmental conditions and selective pressures."

Birds living in the world's cold mountain regions appear to be particularly at risk.

"Populations of species living at high altitudes and in colder places have fewer opportunities to move towards cooler areas or upslope to avoid increasing temperatures, and hence may have increased extinction risk," the paper said.

Another problem is that higher temperatures are inducing birds to lay eggs earlier.

"For animals living in these environments the effects of temperature changes may have been exacerbated, potentially leading to disruption in synchronisation between the timing of chick-feeding and peak food availability," the paper said.

14 February 2017

⇨ The above information is reprinted with kind permission from *The Independent*. Please visit www.independent.co.uk for further information.

Bumblebees risking extinction from neonicotinoid pesticides

Bumblebees are less able to start colonies when exposed to a common neonicotinoid pesticide, which could lead to collapses in wild bee populations, according to new research published today in *Nature Ecology & Evolution*.

Researchers from Royal Holloway, University of London, and the University of Guelph have found that exposure to thiamethoxam, a common pesticide, reduced the chances of a bumblebee queen starting a new colony by more than a quarter. Building on field studies, the researchers used mathematical models of bumblebee populations which showed that thiamethoxam exposure significantly increases the likelihood that wild bee populations could become extinct.

"Queens exposed to the pesticide were 26% less likely to lay eggs to start a colony," said Dr Gemma Baron, from the School of Biological Sciences at Royal Holloway. "Creating new bee colonies is vital for the survival of bumblebees – if queens don't produce eggs or start new colonies it is possible that bumblebees could die out completely."

Neonicotinoid pesticides can stop bees forming new colonies

"Building on previous knowledge, we were able to use mathematical models to show that this reduction in colony founding could lead to a very real threat of extinction in wild bumblebee populations," said Professor Vincent Jansen, also from Royal Holloway. Neonicotinoids are the most widely used class of pesticide in the world. It is vital that we understand the effects of these pesticides on our wildlife."

The EU has issued a temporary ban on the use of thiamethoxam, as well as two other neonicotinoid pesticides. Neonicotinoids have long been implicated In the decline of bees, butterflies and other species, and there is currently global debate about their usage.

Professor Nigel Raine from the University of Guelph commented:

"This research shows that these pesticides can have a devastating effect on bees, and we urgently need to know more about how pesticides could be affecting other species."

Bumblebee queens already face a hugely challenging task if they try to start new colonies. They must first survive the winter, which can cause them to lose up to 80% of their fat reserves, and then surmount the threats posed by parasites, predators, bad weather and a lack of resources. The additional impacts of neonicotinoid pesticides could prove devastating.

Professor Mark Brown, also of Royal Holloway, says "Our work is a major step forward in understanding how pesticides may impact bumblebees and other pollinating species."

This study was funded by a BBSRC-DTG studentship, and the Insect Pollinators Initiative (joint-funded by the Biotechnology and Biological Sciences Research Council, Defra, the Natural Environment Research Council (NERC), the Scottish Government and the Wellcome Trust. It is managed under the auspices of the Living with Environmental Change (LWEC) partnership).

14 August 2017

⇨ The above information is reprinted with kind permission from Royal Holloway University of London. Please visit www.royalholloway.ac.uk for further information.

Warming seas raise hunger threat for seabirds

Seabirds may struggle to find food for their chicks as they are unable to shift their breeding seasons as the climate warms, a study suggests.

Rising sea temperatures in coming decades could create a mismatch between breeding periods and times when prey is most plentiful, researchers say.

The findings suggest that if prey species continue to shift their breeding seasons forward – as previous studies have shown in some regions – it could further threaten the survival of vulnerable seabirds such as puffins and albatrosses.

Breeding habits

A team from The University of Edinburgh, the Centre for Ecology & Hydrology and the British Antarctic Survey studied data on the breeding patterns of 62 seabird species between 1952 and 2016, as sea surface temperatures rose sharply.

They found that seabirds have not altered their breeding times in response to rising temperatures. Previous research has shown however that climate change has brought forward when many prey species – including squid, shrimp and small fish – reproduce.

Seabirds have much longer lifespans than their prey and do not reproduce until they are a few years old, which means it takes them many more generations to adapt, researchers say.

Widespread survey

The team assessed 145 bird populations at 60 locations across every continent. These included the British Antarctic Survey's sub-Antarctic Bird Island Research Station and the Centre for Ecology & Hydrology's field site on the Isle of May in the Firth of Forth.

The study, published in the journal *Nature Climate Change*, received funding from the Natural Environment Research Council.

"Many plants and animals now breed earlier than in previous decades, so our finding that seabirds haven't responded to changing environments is really surprising".

Katharine Keogan
School of Biological Sciences

"This collaboration was a global team effort, bringing together many of the world's seabird scientists and the data they have spent many years collecting. Uniting these studies has allowed us to draw powerful conclusions about the climate response of one of the most vulnerable bird groups on the planet".

Dr Sue Lewis
Centre for Ecology & Hydrology

3 April 2018

⇨ The above information is reprinted with kind permission from The University of Edinburgh. Please visit www.ed.ac.uk for further information.

Dire news for endangered right whales: not a single newborn spotted this year

"Right now, the sky is falling," warns a National Marine Fisheries Service scientist.

By Mary Papenfuss

Endangered North Atlantic right whales are facing an increasingly bleak future as researchers report they haven't spotted any new calves this season.

Trained spotters look for newborns from December to the end of March by flying over the coasts of Florida and Georgia, where female right whales typically give birth. If they don't see any new calves by next Saturday, it will be the first time since 1989 that newborns haven't been found.

Barb Zoodsma, who oversees the right whale recovery programme in the U.S. Southeast for the National Marine Fisheries Service, told the Associated Press that the dearth of calves could signal the "beginning of the end" for the species.

"Right now, the sky is falling," Zoodsma said. "I do think we can turn this around. But. . . what's our willpower to do so? This is a time for all hands on deck."

Spotters were already alarmed in December by the lack of female right whales off the southeastern U.S. coast, National Public Radio reported. The whales typically live off New England and Canada, but pregnant females head south starting in November to give birth and raise their calves in warmer water. But this year, spotters didn't see any females in the south until the end of January.

Only about 450 North Atlantic right whales exist, and only 100 of them are breeding females. 17 of the animals washed up dead in 2017, and one was found this year. Many were struck by ships or entangled in fishing line, including line between floating buoys and lobster traps. The line can cut through the whales' fins, cause infections and drag them down, sapping their strength.

Only five newborns were spotted during calving season in 2017. The whales typically average about 17 births a year.

Some scientists are holding out hope that the mothers have shifted their locations and that calves might be somewhere spotters aren't looking – or that the births may rebound in the future.

But many researchers fear that the species is being decimated by ship strikes, fishing line and climate change. The whales feed on phytoplankton, which is temperature-sensitive. As water temperatures increase off New England, the phytoplankton population is decreasing.

27 March 2018

⇨ The above information is reprinted with kind permission from The Huffington Post UK. Please visit www.huffingtonpost.co.uk for further information.

Time running out for cheetahs as scientists fear for future of world's fastest land animal

A new review of cheetah populations in southern Africa suggests there are far fewer of the animals than previously thought.

By Aristos Georgiou

A new review of cheetah populations has revealed the dire state one of the planet's most iconic big cats and the world's fastest land animal that can reach speeds of 70mph, prompting calls by scientists to place the species on the International Union for Conservation of Nature's (IUCN) Red List of 'Endangered' species.

An international team of researchers argue that low cheetah population estimates in southern Africa and population decline warrant a downgrade from its present 'Vulnerable' status.

For the study, published in the journal *PeerJ*, researchers analysed cheetah numbers over six years in an 800,000-square-kilometre region that stretches across Namibia, Botswana, and South Africa.

"This is the area with the largest population of free-ranging cheetahs left on Earth. Knowing how many cheetahs there are and where they occur is crucial for developing suitable conservation management plans for the species," said Varsha Vijay from Duke University.

They found that only 3,577 adult cheetahs lived in the vast region, which is larger than France, while 55% of individual animals were found in just two habitats. These estimates are 11% lower than the IUCN's current assessment.

"This collaborative, multiyear effort sounds the alarm about the state of cheetah populations in southern Africa, shining a light on the imperative need to protect these majestic predators," said Gary E. Knell, President and CEO

of the National Geographic Society, who supported the research.

The study also estimated the number of cheetahs in areas where it is possible for the animals to live but there had been no confirmed sightings.

"To better understand this rare and elusive species, we need to complement the monitoring of confirmed populations with the investigation of possible cheetah habitat," said Vijay.

Furthermore, the research found that only around 18% of the cheetah's range is within internationally recognized protected areas. The majority of the animals roam across private land that is mostly used for livestock and game production.

Some farmers who share land with cheetahs actively persecute them, which can lead to population declines, according to the study.

"The future of the cheetah relies heavily on working with farmers who host these big cats on their lands, bearing the heaviest cost of coexistence," said Florian Weise from the Claws Conservancy.

By listing the cheetah as 'Endangered', more awareness would be created about its precarious situation, opening up more avenues for funding that could go towards conservation and population monitoring efforts, the researchers say.

11 December 2017

⇨ The above information is reprinted with kind permission from *International Business Times*. Please visit www.ibtimes.co.uk for further information.

Study investigates impact of lions living alongside giraffe populations

New research from the University of Bristol is calling for an urgent review into how populations of giraffes are managed in the wild when living alongside lions.

It is commonly accepted that lions are the only predators to pose a risk to giraffes on an individual basis but there has never been a study to investigate how the presence of lions impacts on the population as a whole.

Now, in the first study of its kind, published today in the journal *PLOS One*, Bristol PhD student Zoe Muller has found that if lions are kept in the same conservation area as giraffes, the number of calves is likely to be reduced, maybe by as much as 82 per cent.

Zoe, based at the University's School of Biological Sciences, said: "It is thought that lions preferentially target giraffe calves in the wild, and there is anecdotal evidence of this, including observations of lions eating young giraffe carcasses and of lion claw marks on adult females (thought to be a result of them defending their calves).

"However, no-one has ever investigated if this preference for hunting calves has an impact on the population as a whole."

This study investigates how the population demography of giraffes differs between two adjacent sites – one with no lions, and one with a high density of lions, and found that the presence of lions has a significant impact on the demography of giraffe populations.

In areas containing no lions, the giraffe population contained 34 per cent of juveniles (individuals less than a year old) but in the presence of lions it only contained six per cent juveniles.

Giraffe populations have declined by 40 per cent in the last 30 years, and there are now thought to be fewer than 98,000 individuals remaining in the wild.

In recognition of their drastic decline in the wild, they have recently been listed as 'Vulnerable' on the International Union for Conservation in Nature's Red List of Threatened Species.

However, conservation review is ongoing due to current debate over their taxonomic status, since some subspecies may be even more at risk of extinction than is currently recognised.

Zoe added: "This research has significant practical implications. Giraffes are a threatened species, suffering ongoing decline in the wild, and this research highlights how managing giraffes alongside lions inside a conservation area (a common practice in Africa) has detrimental effects for giraffe populations.

"The continual loss of juveniles within a population due to lion predation may lead to an unrecoverable situation where the population crashes, since population growth and sustainability rely on enough calves surviving until they are sexually mature.

"This research highlights the need for an urgent reassessment of how populations of giraffes are managed in the wild, given their Vulnerable Red List status and severe and ongoing decline."

The next steps for this research will be to replicate the findings in other areas of Africa. This is one case study from East Africa, and more research is needed to see if lions create the same effects in other giraffe populations.

3 January 2018

⇨ The above information is reprinted with kind permission from the University of Bristol. Please visit www.bristol.ac.uk for further information.

Pangolins: why this cute prehistoric mammal is facing extinction

The pangolin's body armour protects it from all known predators – except man. Martin Fletcher travels to Vietnam, where the unique animal is being eaten to extinction.

A what? A pangolin. It's the only mammal in the world that is completely covered in scales. It looks like an artichoke on legs. Or a cross between a crocodile and a snake. Or a wacky computer-game invention.

It is one of ten animals that Sir David Attenborough would put on his personal ark, and with good reason. It is 80 million years old (*Homo sapiens* is a mere eight). It eats 200,000 ants and termites a day. It has a (sticky) tongue almost as long as its body and stores stones in its stomach to grind up food. When threatened it rolls itself up into an armour-plated ball that protects it from all known predators. Except, unfortunately, humans. They simply pick up the balls and take them away – on such a scale that pangolins have become the world's most trafficked mammal.

Each year about 100,000 are snatched from the wild and shipped to China and Vietnam, where their meat is considered a delicacy, their scales allegedly "cure" anything from acne to cancer, and they fetch several hundred dollars each. The demand has soared as those countries have boomed economically. Pangolins are being traded on an "epic scale", the International Union for the Conservation of Nature (IUCN) says. They are in "precipitous decline", have been "extirpated from vast areas" of south-east Asia and are increasingly being plundered in Africa. All eight varieties of pangolin feature on the IUCN's Red List of animals threatened with extinction, and two are critically endangered.

As the Duke of Cambridge noted recently, "The humble pangolin… runs the risk of becoming extinct before most of us have even heard of it."

It was time, I decided, to check them out. I would have gone to a zoo, except that pangolins seldom survive in captivity and not a single British zoo possesses any (Leipzig is the only zoo in Europe, and one of only six in the world, that does). That – along with the fact that pangolins are shy and nocturnal, and were ignored by Rudyard Kipling and Walt Disney, and lack the celebrity status of elephants, rhinos and tigers – helps explain why so few westerners even realise they exist.

So I went to Vietnam, though the Vietnamese Government refused me a journalist's visa when I explained why I wanted to go. I took an overnight flight to Bangkok, a dawn connection to Hanoi and – having sneaked in as a tourist – a taxi down to the Cuc Phuong national park, where a plucky little NGO called Save Vietnam's Wildlife (SVW) runs a pangolin rescue and rehabilitation centre.

I never reached the park that day. Nguyen Van Thai, the determined young man who runs SVW, called as my taxi was still battling Hanoi's millions of motor scooters. The authorities had confiscated four pangolins from traffickers on the Chinese border, he said. I could go and fetch them with him – 250 miles; eight more hours of travelling. Wonderful, I replied, as I fought the urge to sleep.

All day we drove north through the towns and cities of this teeming nation, past spiky little mountains and lush green paddy fields, stopping only for a meal of tripe and fermented cabbage with rice in a roadside cafe (I opted for an omelette).

We reached the city of Ha Giang long after dark. There, officials from the Forest Protection Department (FPD) pulled a flimsy wooden box from a garage. Thai prised it open with a machete, releasing a powerful stench of cooped-up animal and excrement. Inside were three plastic sacks and one net bag, each containing a brownish-

black ball roughly the size and weight of a curling stone.

He placed the balls on the ground. Gradually, and with great caution, one began to uncurl, revealing a blackcurrant eye, a long pointed snout and a body with a soft pink underbelly that tapered into an even longer tail. The pangolin tried repeatedly to stand up, but was so weak it kept toppling over. By the morning, to Thai's distress, it was dead.

Thai explained that two motorcyclists had been caught the previous week as they crossed into China along a forest track at dawn. The pangolins were in their backpacks. He had read of the incident in a newspaper, but it had taken him five days to secure the FPD's permission to take the animals away. The rangers had evidently not thought to remove them from their sacks during that time or to give them food and water. "They don't care very much about wildlife. They're only interested in saving trees," Thai observed.

The next day, as we returned to Cuc Phuong with the three surviving animals in the boot, Thai expanded on the pangolin's plight. As a boy growing up near the national park in the late 1980s he used to see them all the time, he said, but none had been spotted in its 54,000 acres since 2006. After they had been hunted almost to extinction throughout northern Vietnam and southern China, they began to be imported in industrial quantities from Malaysia, Indonesia and other parts of south-east Asia, though international trade in pangolins was effectively banned in 2000. Now, in an alarming sign that south-east Asia's pangolins are running out, scales are starting to arrive in large shipments from Africa.

The pangolins are caught in their forest lairs with nets or snares or dogs, Thai explained. They are smuggled into Vietnam by land from Laos, or by ship to Haiphong port – dead and alive, fresh and frozen, gutted, skinned, disguised as fish or snakes and in loads weighing as much as 20 tons. They are then spirited in lorries, trains, buses, taxis and even ambulances to Hanoi or Ho Chi Minh City, or on to China where they command even higher prices than in Vietnam. Before selling them, the traffickers frequently pump their stomachs full of gravel or rice starch, or inject water between their scales and flesh, to increase their weight and hence their value.

Sometimes traffickers are caught, Thai said, but seldom because of assiduous policing. Usually rivals have snitched on them or an informant has betrayed them for money. Some traffickers escape punishment by bribing the police. Others are fined according to the weight of the haul. But they are hardly ever imprisoned.

Moreover, a legal loophole allows the police to sell some confiscated pangolins on the open market and to keep the proceeds. The police have even been known to sell pangolins back to the very traffickers they seized them from. "It's terrible," Thai said.

When we eventually reached Cuc Phuong that second night, Thai showed me SVW's 'pangolarium' where ten pangolins are kept in large wire-mesh cages in a tranquil wooded compound on the edge of the national park until they can be safely restored to the wild.

"I love pangolins. They're very special," Thai said. And anyone who has come into contact with them agrees. Jonathan Baillie, the head of conservation programmes at the Zoological Society of London, describes them as "amazing, wonderful creatures". Attenborough calls them "one of the most endearing animals I have ever met", and it is not hard to see why they inspire such affection.

Pangolins are solitary animals but don't mind being picked up. They are strong but gentle and placid and have no teeth. They carry their young on their tails and curl round them to protect them. They use their prehensile tails to swing from branches, and they stretch out horizontally to reach ant nests. They walk with a slightly comic rolling gait. They have poor sight but a very good sense of smell and they emit little sneezing noises when they sense food. They are intelligent and have distinct personalities. Some are friendly, others timid. Some are lazy, others active. Some are determined escapologists.

A particularly outgoing pangolin called Lucky is everyone's favourite. She earned her name when the authorities offered the rescue centre five pangolins after discovering 72 on a truck. Thai went to collect them but found one of the five had died. "I said, "Can I change it for a live one?' " he recalls, "and they said, Yes, but you have to choose a small one,' as they wanted to sell the others. So I picked up Lucky and the rest got eaten."

Another remarkable thing about pangolins is how little is known about them. Dan Challender, who co-chairs the IUCN's pangolin specialist group with Baillie, calls them "the forgotten species". Some live in trees, others in burrows, but nobody is certain whether they stay in one place, how they mate, how long they take to gestate, how long they live or exactly what they eat. Thai's rescue centre has settled on a diet of ants, silkworm larvae and soy beans. It manages to keep more of its pangolins alive than most other places, though many arrive so weak and traumatised by their abductions that they die within a day or two.

Nor does anyone know how many pangolins are left, though a million are thought to have been killed in the past decade. Of the four types found in Asia, the Chinese and Sunda pangolins are deemed to be 'critically endangered', and the Indian and Philippine pangolins 'endangered'. The four African species are all rated as 'vulnerable', but they are increasingly being targeted as Asia's pangolin populations shrivel. In July, for example, Vietnamese customs officials seized 1.4 tons of pangolin scales, the product of roughly 3,000 animals, from a cargo ship arriving from Sierra Leone.

"The African markets are now being ignited," Baillie told me. "In the past you didn't see any traffic from Africa, and you wouldn't go all that way to ship them back if you had a sufficient supply of your own."

Vietnam has a poor conservation record. Its last Javan rhino was poached in the Cat Tien national park in 2010. The regime now claims to be stepping up its efforts to combat the trade in pangolins, and has promised to upgrade them to the highest level of protection. But Thai and I saw little sign of that when we visited Hanoi at the end of my trip. Buying – or pretending to buy – pangolin products in the Vietnamese capital proved as easy as the practice was abhorrent.

In the space of two hours we visited four traditional medicine shops in the bustling Old Quarter and found pangolin scales on sale in three of them.

The first, in Thuoc Bac Street, had a packet of powdered scales labelled te-te (pangolin) displayed on its front counter, and the middle-aged woman who ran it produced a sweet jar full of untreated scales from the back of the shop when we asked. The scales cured cancer, poor circulation and arthritis, she assured us before demanding $1,100 a kilo. I asked her why they were so expensive. "Because they're rare and illegal," she replied, without a trace of shame.

In the second shop, on Hang Vai Street, the manageress moved aside a plastic container full of some innocuous herb to reveal one plastic bag of untreated scales and another of fried scales. She wanted $1,500 a kilo, but lowered the price to $1,250. She claimed pangolin scales cured cancer and improved a mother's lactation, and she even wrote down the Vietnamese word for pangolin on her business card so I could check for myself online.

In the fourth shop, on Lan Ong Street, the assistant produced a bag full of untreated scales from a small drawer at the back of her premises. Asked how to prepare them, she advised microwaving them then putting them in a blender, before serving the resulting powder in a soup. She wanted only $750 a kilo.

I sensed Thai's disgust, but he said that reporting the shops to the authorities was pointless because they would do nothing. "They really don't care once the animals are dead," he complained. Indeed, the official handbook of Vietnamese traditional medicine still openly commends pangolin scales as a remedy for "stimulating energy and blood circulation, destroying ulcers and promoting milk secretion in the human body", and for treating "ulcerated scrofula" and "acnes". It even

gives detailed recipes for treating each ailment. It is all nonsense, of course. Pangolin scales are made of keratin, like human hair and finger nails, and have no medicinal value whatsoever.

To find restaurants that served pangolin meat, we drove across the broad Red River to Hanoi's Long Bien district and pretended to be looking for somewhere to entertain some friends that night.

The upmarket Tran Ban restaurant offers diners "the traditional taste of the countryside". Its menu lists all sorts of wild meats – porcupine, civet, boar, swan, turtle, cobra, rattlesnake and, of course, pangolin. There is even a picture of one. A keen young waiter said a live pangolin would cost $250 a kilo and take a couple of days to acquire. Its throat would be slit at our table and its blood added to our wine. The meat could be stir-fried, steamed or cooked with spices.

The equally smart Huong Que restaurant promised us all that and more. Its ornate reception area was decorated with outsized jars of rice wine in which various animals were slowly pickling: king cobras, geckos, lizards. The menu offered us pangolin in various forms: steamed, grilled, 'half-done browned in fat', 'carefully cooked with Chinese medicinal herbs', 'stir-fried puddings', 'simmer bone porridge' or 'a whole one was steamed' (sic).

The beaming manager poured us green tea. He said he would need a few hours' notice to procure a pangolin but could get one for that night. It would cost $250 a kilo. He recommended steaming it, with the tongue chopped into pieces for a soup. He promised we could watch its throat being slit and claimed the blood was an aphrodisiac. He then produced from a back room a large jar of rice wine with a small, dead pangolin floating in it – a truly grotesque sight. He offered us that as well for another $200.

Thai was seething. Selling pangolins is simply not considered a serious offence in Vietnam, he protested. "The authorities all know of places like this but they don't want to do anything about them." The problem was not the poor and uneducated, he continued, but the elite – the senior government

officials and wealthy businessmen who order pangolin to flaunt their status. "90 million Vietnamese can no longer see pangolins in their own country because a few rich officials and businessmen want to eat them. I think that's disgusting."

Baillie agrees. "In the 21st century we should not be eating species to extinction. There is no excuse for allowing this illegal trade to continue." And so does Chris Shepherd, regional director for south-east Asia of the wildlife watchdog Traffic. "Sadly most law-enforcement agencies don't view pangolins as a high priority. Basically we either increase enforcement or kiss pangolins goodbye," he says.

Thai does his best to raise awareness of the pangolin's plight in Vietnam, but with an annual budget of just $35,000, raised entirely from foreign donors, SVW can only do so much. Outside pressure is needed, and that is belatedly beginning to build. In 2013, the first global conference on pangolin conservation was held in Singapore. Last year the IUCN's newly formed pangolin specialist group published a detailed action plan. Baillie is now trying to persuade children's writers and artists to popularise the animal, and in November the Duke of Cambridge brought his star power to bear by launching a version of the Angry Birds game featuring pangolins.

Having now seen pangolins for myself, I am a convert to the cause. They are a creature like no other, one of nature's curiosities, and the world would be poorer without them. But I must make a confession: I have eaten pangolin myself. I did so in the company of three French helicopter pilots whom I met in the Gabonese town of Oyem in 2013. I do not remember the meat tasting very special, and my only defence is that I was unaware at the time of the threat to pangolins. I know better now.

31 January 2015

How people can live next to lions without killing them – new study

An article from **The Conversation.**

THE CONVERSATION

By Grant Hopcraft, Research Fellow, University of Glasgow and assisted by Sarah Blackburn, MSc student in biodiversity and conservation.

There is a sense of haunting to the roar of a lion veiled in darkness. The emphatic "ooooaa!" demands attention as it starts in the abdomen and reverberates through the night air. Its direction and distance are secondary to one's primordial reaction – a sudden dilation of the pupils and a flare of prickles on the neck. The call unmistakably announces a large carnivore, yet as each roar fades into solitary grunts it feels less like an act of aggression than the lonely imploring of a lost soul in the darkness.

The plight of Africa's lions is lamentable. Since the 1960s, the world has lost at least 70% of these magnificent cats, which until a few thousand years ago inhabited most of Europe, Asia and the Americas. Now we're down to around 20,000, all of them in Africa apart from one sub-species in India. Habitat loss and the encroachment of people are largely responsible – lions in Kenya and Tanzania are shot by wildlife officials if they consistently kill livestock, for instance. And trophy hunters still shoot lions in the wild every year in countries where it is permitted, including Tanzania and Zimbabwe.

But if you were expecting a fable in which cunning Human steals from noble Lion, this story is not so clear-cut. Living with these predators is not easy. For many people in rural Africa, livestock pay for school fees and hospital bills, and insure against

misfortune. Imagine finding half your nest egg has been taken overnight and, worse, worrying your family might be next. Unsurprisingly, many lions that live near people end up shot or poisoned. Yet it doesn't have to be this way. A new five-year study that I have been involved in shows that when people directly benefit from lions, they become more tolerant of their faults.

Conservancies

We focused on an area surrounding the Mara National Reserve in Kenya, a protected zone at the northern extent of the Serengeti ecosystem. These fertile grasslands are the home of the Maasai, semi-nomadic pastoralists who share them with the great annual migration of over a million wildebeest and their predators, including lions.

Maasai have always speared any rogue that dares interfere with their livestock; and today there are far more people and livestock and much less space for lions. Yet many on the northern edge of the Mara have wisely noted the premiums that tourists are prepared to pay for the Serengeti experience.

Lions help attract over 350,000 visitors to the area every year, generating $90 million (£63 million) in entrance fees alone. Beyond the national reserve, many families have combined landholdings into community conservancies which welcome visitors for a fee. They attract wildlife by

managing and protecting resources such as livestock, water and unique habitats; and they distribute income fairly around the community to avoid feuds. Other families have declined this opportunity, relying purely on their livestock for income.

Hence there is a 1,500sqkm patchwork of conservancies and other privately owned pastureland to the north of the Mara National Reserve. Together with the reserve itself, where no one lives and lions can roam freely, it amounts to a perfect three-way natural experiment to investigate the effects of conservancies on lions. Sara Blackburn and Laurence Frank, a veteran predator biologist, spent five years observing the lifespan of 382 lions in the area. This is the first time anyone has looked at the survival rates of individual lions in relation to conservancies, rather than just counting them.

The natural life expectancy of a lion living in the wild rarely exceeds 13 years. When we compared the survival of lions living outside national parks, our results consistently showed that survival is not determined by how many prey are available or the quality of the habitat – there are enough of both to sustain this population. The number of livestock in a lion's territory makes no difference either.

The only factor that consistently cuts short a lion's life, sometimes lowering the chances of survival by as much as 40%, is the number of homesteads in its territory that are not part of a community conservancy. Homesteads that are members of a conservancy, on the other hand, have no negative effect on lions' survival chances. This suggests that when people receive income from lions via ecotourism, they become tolerant and lions survive. There is a good chance that the same would also be true for other animals that are declining across the region, such as giraffe and impala.

Next steps

Cecil, the lion shot by an American hunter last year, drew a line in the sand regarding the public's opinion on conservation of this remarkable predator. These events have sparked heated debates about the role of trophy hunting and using fences to protect lions in the wild, even while recent footage of an agitated lion walking the streets of Nairobi highlights the continued struggle for space.

In this worrying context, our research points to how this story can end more happily. Community conservancies are a viable and working alternative to protecting wildlife. Although they exist in many parts of Kenya and Tanzania, we must continue encouraging governments to develop similar opportunities for local communities to benefit from wildlife through ecotourism. Evidence such as ours gives reason to be optimistic that community conservancies will continue to expand and benefit human and lion alike.

23 March 2016

⇨ The above information is reprinted with kind permission from *The Conversation*. Please visit www. theconversation.com for further information.

Inside the frozen zoo where eggs and sperm are stored to help endangered animals

At San Diego's Frozen Zoo, the cells of thousands of dead animals are preserved in the hope they could help save endangered species.

By Laurence Cornet

In a modest room no larger than 20sq m, many thousands of animals, from the Cuban crocodile to the Hawaiian honeycreeper, lay carefully preserved in liquid nitrogen. "There is no place on Earth where there is so much living material from so many species," says Dr Oliver Ryder, pointing to some storage tanks. "It's the most biodiverse place on the planet."

The 'Frozen Zoo' at San Diego Zoo in southern California houses sperm, eggs and genetic material from more than 10,000 dead animals in total, safeguarded for posterity to preserve genetic diversity, and in the hope that scientists might be able to help save endangered species, or even one day reintroduce species that have long been extinct.

Dr Kurt Benirschke, a pathologist and geneticist, founded the Center for the Reproduction of Endangered Species at the San Diego Zoo in the early 1970s. It was the first research department of its kind, established to study the chromosomes of mammals and particularly those aspects relating to reproduction and evolution.

Dr Ryder, then a young molecular biologist, joined Dr Benirschke at the zoo in 1975, and the pair's focus turned to applying molecular genetics to endangered species.

"At the time, you didn't hear anybody within the academic world talk about conservation," Dr Ryder remembers. "There was a lot that could be done and it was just going be a challenge to figure it out."

Benirschke and Ryder collected the cells and reproductive material of highly endangered species for cryopreservation, with little idea of quite how they could be used in the future. Today that collection, amassed over 40 years, has come to constitute perhaps the richest genetic resource on Earth, comprising cell samples from some 1,000 species and subspecies of mammals, birds, reptiles and amphibians. It will soon add its first insect.

Mighty mouse

When we arrive at the facility, Dr Marisa Korody, senior research associate in genetics, is chopping up the ears of a recently deceased Pacific pocket mouse into 1mm chunks. The animal was a 'founder': caught in the wild, and thus possessing more valuable genes, ones not diluted by captivity.

In the cell culture lab, Dr Korody incubates the chunks of mouse matter for six hours, mixing them with an enzyme that digests the tissues and liberates the cells. The cells will next be kept here to grow – a process that takes anywhere from three weeks to more than a year, depending on the individual specimen. While we are in the lab, the cells of gorillas and southern white rhinos sit developing on the shelves.

Back in the main room, Nicole Ravida, senior research coordinator in reproductive physiology, is slowly freezing the mouse's testicles. The loud ticking of a timer almost drowns out the voice of Marlys L. Houck, senior researcher in genetics, who guides us around the facility. As Houck opens the metal tank containing the frozen cells, it releases the roaring sound of a pressure cooker. She pulls out a samples rack in a cloud of nitrogen, and carefully extracts a 100-vial box. Inside the tiny flasks, beneath colourful corks, are the cells of a Micronesian kingfisher, a Cuban crocodile, an African elephant, a koala and a dik-dik, the smallest antelope on Earth. There are also the cells of an extinct species of bird, the Hawaiian honeycreeper.

The frozen zoo – San Diego's is not the only one – arose from the demise of zoological parks. Once the most lucrative public attraction, zoos lost their appeal as a reluctant visiting public started to develop ethical issues about animal captivity as entertainment. Zoos were thus required to become pioneers in zoological research to remain legitimate and sustainable.

Dr Ryder's first revelation happened in the 1980s, when the American Society of Human Genetics hosted the presentation of a PhD researcher who demonstrated that one could take a hair and genotype it (determine its genetic makeup). Though the presenter was foreseeing the forensic applications of her discovery, Dr Ryder used it to perform the first studies on wild mountain gorillas, which was a controversial subject at the time.

Hello Dolly

Then in 1996, the world's 'holy cow!' moment arrived: Dolly the sheep was born in Edinburgh – the first mammal born from somatic cell nuclear transfer (SCNT), popularly known as cloning.

"You talk about changing your opinion – you really have to do this in science – and I was trained to accept the dogma that once the cells are differentiated, they could not be de-differentiated," says Dr Ryder. "I didn't even want to discuss ideas about using cells in the frozen zoo to recreate animals because I thought it was a sensationalist diversion."

Yet Dolly proved that it was possible to take a single cell and ultimately produce a functional animal capable of reproducing itself. The zoo later made auspicious discoveries around the ability to reprogramme a cell: to take it from its developed stage – a skin cell or a nerve cell – and make it become pluripotent (able to make any cell in the body).

"That was outstanding when you think that we have possibly the world's most diverse collection of stem cells," says Dr Ryder.

This inevitably leads to delicate questions about their use. Dr Ryder's position is to avoid molecular cell transfer unless it is absolutely necessary. Cloning, he says, comes with a series of consequences that haven't been studied enough yet. (The San Diego zoo performed cloning once, in 2003. The successful experiment resulted in the birth of a banteng – a species of wild cattle found in South-east Asia.)

Reintroduction to the wild is another major challenge for the zoo, especially for species of amphibians that are kept in captivity in environments very different from their natural habitat.

"Historically, it was underestimated how big a problem reintroduction was," says Dr Ryder. "But it is amenable to some research. The problem is that we are in a race against time. Some of these species are not surviving in the wild and our only choice for saving them sometimes involves these very intensive technologies."

Getting the horn

This is striking when we look at efforts directed towards the protection of northern white rhinos, the zoo's principal cause. In Kenya, at the Ol Pejeta Conservancy, adequate protection requires heavily armed anti-poaching militias watching over the animals 24/7. For less critical subspecies, preventive measures consist of immobilising animals and cutting off their horns in order to discourage ivory hunters.

At San Diego, it's another kind of immobilisation. The three remaining northern white rhinos are too old to reproduce naturally and the only alternative to avoid their extinction is to make use of assisted reproductive techniques, with a female southern white rhino as surrogate. Using cells from their collection, they have sequenced the genomes of the cells of both subspecies and determined that they are compatible. Still, it's an ambitious undertaking.

"It's unprecedented. We will have to do embryo transfers, which we have never done on rhinos, but every

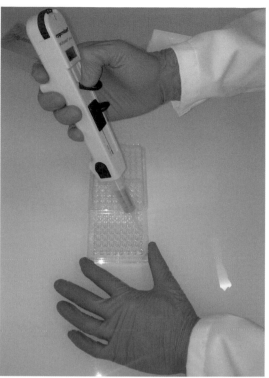

step we have taken on rhinos is not a fantasy, it's an activity that's been done with other mammals," Dr Ryder says.

Methods may differ, yet on each continent conservationists aim to adjust an animal to enable it to survive in today's wild environment, where space is ever more scarce and hostile. So, what do we want for the future?

"The choice to bring species back from the brink of extinction one species at a time," says Dr Ryder, "may not be a solution that everyone sees as perfect. But it might be a solution that most people will appreciate is the right thing to do at this time.

"We sit here today and guess about this, and we will probably be wrong. One thing I am pretty sure about, though, is that if we save cells, we will have a lot more opportunities and options. If we can keep them for a long time, we will change the potential of the biodiversity of the planet."

4 May 2016

⇨ The above information is reprinted with kind permission from inews. Please visit www.inews.co.uk for further information.

Devil rays receive new protection

New regulations will be in force from the 4th April 2017!

By Jane Hosegood

The highly threatened devil ray has received a new level of protection at a recent international meeting on wildlife trade.

People's Trust for Endangered Species (PTES) grantee Jane Hosegood updated us on this latest good news after attending the Convention on the International Trade in Endangered Species (CITES) meeting in Johannesburg. She is an expert in ray genetics and current leads a PTES-funded study with the aim of developing genetic tools for their conservation.

Protecting the devil rays!

Both the devil rays, and their sister group, the Manta rays, are fished in huge numbers to supply the international demand for their gill plates, which are used as a pseudo-remedy in some traditional medicines, despite no evidence that they provide any real health benefit. This trade is unsustainable, as these species have a very slow reproductive rate, and so are unable to recover from exploitation. Sadly, as a result, major declines have been reported in many populations around the world.

But some good news has recently come out of a large international meeting on wildlife trade. All nine species of devil ray, are to join their close relatives, the Manta rays, on Appendix II of the Convention on the International Trade in Endangered Species (CITES), following the success of a proposal submitted by the Government of Fiji. 183 countries are signatories to CITES, and will now be required to regulate and monitor trade in gill plates, or any other parts or derivatives of these species. Similar protection was also agreed for silky and thresher sharks.

I was lucky enough to attend the recent CITES meeting in Johannesburg alongside colleagues from the Manta Trust and TRACE Wildlife Forensics Network, and so saw first-hand how events unfolded. Despite some discussions of concerns regarding enforcement of the proposed listings, the devil ray proposal was a success, receiving the required two-thirds majority vote from government delegations from the signatory countries. This listing will come into effect later this year.

It was really great to see 4,000 people, mostly government officials, from all over the world coming together to discuss issues of trade in wildlife products, from elephants to pangolins, parrots to sharks, and of course, the 'mini mantas' or devil rays.

The fact that the devil rays are now to be regulated under CITES is excellent news. It is not just beneficial for the devils – but Mantas too. Mantas were listed in 2013, and so trade in Manta parts has been regulated for the last few years. However, due to difficulties identifying between gill plates of different species, specialist training was required to distinguish between listed manta parts, and unregulated devil ray parts. In light of the recent resolutions for the devil rays, all gill plates are now regulated, and so it is no longer possible to hide manta gill plates among devil ray gill plates in trade. Not only that, but the new listings allow for more stringent and standardised monitoring of the trade, and is therefore a massive step forward for marine conservation.

My work focuses on developing genetic tools for the conservation of Manta and devil rays, and so this new listing is very relevant for me. The conference was a fantastic opportunity for me to talk to people from around the world about how my science could be used to help with problems faced when implementing regulations such as CITES. One of the main problems surrounding manta and devil rays on CITES is identifying which species a gill plate came from. It's very clear that high up on the wish list of those on the frontline against the illegal wildlife trade is some sort of tool to help them quickly, easily and cheaply identify a wildlife product to species level. Fortunately, this is exactly what I've been working towards for Manta and devil rays for the last couple of years, with the help of generous support from PTES.

Essentially what we are doing is taking tissue samples from individuals of known species and sequencing short fragments of the DNA that they contain. This allows us to build up a picture of the genetic signatures of each species and population, to which we can compare samples from an unknown individual or part. This could therefore be used to figure out which species an illegal gill plate came from, and allow us to collect data on which species and regions are most targeted for this purpose. I am currently spending my time analysing the genetic data I've been sequencing from devil ray species, as well as Mantas.

It was absolutely incredible to be in the room witnessing such an important decision to regulate trade in devil ray parts, and this has spurred me to work even harder to protect these species, and to celebrate the conservation successes!

4 April 2017

⇨ The above information iss reprinted with kind permission from People's Trust for Endangered Species. Please visit www.ptes.org for further information.

Some thoughts on 'rewilding'...

Compiled with the input of staff from The Wildlife Trust.

The publication of a new book promoting the idea of rewilding has already stimulated a welcome public debate about why and how land is managed for nature. The author of *Feral*, George Monbiot, argues that "optimising the diversity of the web of life" can be achieved by humans stepping back from nature – letting it go "feral". He also raises questions about how conservation is practised. Why are trees cut down in the lowlands? Why is land grazed in the uplands? Surely we should just let it all be natural without us?

Many will feel kinship with Monbiot's love of the wild and would agree that rewilding is an extremely attractive proposition. Indeed, encouraging nature to flourish and working to restore degraded wild places is why The Wildlife Trusts exist. At sea, we have been vocal in campaigning for Marine Conservation Zones, protected areas which would allow our seas to recover and be 'rewilded'.

The state of nature

Humans have had an impact on our landscape in Britain for at least 7,000 years. You only have to read the new State of Nature report, compiled by the RSPB, The Wildlife Trusts and many other NGOs to understand that we live on a highly-developed island where nature and wilderness struggles to survive. For a long time, people, for better or worse, have been part of the ecology of our landscape. The Wildlife Trusts are working hard to repair the damage that has been done so that nature can recover, but, even if we are aiming to restore natural processes and re-establish wildness where we can, there are still places where retaining some special habitats and the wildlife they support requires some human intervention.

Around half of our terrestrial species live in open habitats which require some sort of natural disturbance (or management intervention by humans) to exist – and which ultimately would be at risk of extinction with no type of management at all. With humans already culpable for such great losses of species and habitats we have to ask ourselves – with the ability to save and restore wildlife – have we reached the position where are we ready to let go and almost certainly lose much more?

Our natural heritage

Ideally wildlife would not need such active intervention to thrive but the reality is that for now in some places we don't have that luxury. Nature reserves are named this way for a reason. They are reserves for the future – not the answer in themselves. Our wildlife has retreated into these last strongholds, and to give us a chance of one day expanding them and helping wildlife to disperse and recolonise, we must first of all preserve the diversity within them. This can involve sustaining traditional land management practices to maintain the richness of our wildflower meadows, woodlands or heathlands – places that are part of our natural and cultural heritage. But on some nature reserves this can mean minimal or no management at all, or a mixture of approaches.

Restoring nature

Meanwhile – and this is the breakthrough that The Wildlife Trusts and others have made – whole new areas of land need to be made more hospitable for wildlife and natural processes restored. Our vision is for Living Landscapes which give so much more space for nature that there would much less need for human intervention to maintain diversity.

With this ambition The Wildlife Trusts are re-naturalising rivers, working with farmers to create wildlife habitats in highly modified landscapes, reintroducing keystone species like the beaver to Scotland and blocking hundreds of kilometres of drainage ditches dug across our uplands to restore their hydrology and wildlife. The restoration of natural processes often involves initial work to reverse damage (e.g. reprofiling a river bank to restore it to its natural state) and then standing back to let nature do the rest. The latter example is also a good example of conservation providing benefits that help nature to show up on the country's balance sheet – in this case through the value of (drinking) water and carbon storage. We can only hope for diversity to be sustained if we can achieve this type of restoration on a decent scale.

Rewilding ourselves

But this is also about the relationship between humans and the rest of the natural world. People need to understand that they are part of, not separate to, nature. Until this happens on a significant scale the odds will always be stacked against us. Our task is to create a rich new ecology for the future and we believe that humans must be part of this. All this takes time, effort and money of course. The support of our members helps us to achieve a massive amount but funding streams such as those that deliver agri-environment schemes are also critical. Just as important is the political will to get behind fantastic restoration ideas like the Great Fen project in the Cambridgeshire fens or the Pumlumon Project in Wales. That same will should reject those proposals – such as the plan to build a new M4 'relief' road across the wetlands of the Gwent Levels – that are out of kilter with saving, let alone improving, nature's fortunes.

⇨   The above information is reprinted with kind permission from The Wildlife Trusts. Please visit www.wildlifetrusts.org for further information.

© 2018 The Wildlife Trusts

Innovative licence issued to help hen harrier

Action forms part of the Defra Hen Harrier Recovery Plan.

Natural England has today issued a licence permitting the trial of a brood management scheme of hen harriers with the long-term aim of increasing their numbers across England.

The licence is time-limited for a two-year period and places stringent conditions on the trial, which will take place in the northern uplands of England. Brood management will only take place with the permission of the land owner.

Brood management is the sixth action within the Defra Hen Harrier Recovery Plan, ultimately aiming to reduce hen harrier predation of grouse chicks on driven grouse moors, leading to an improvement in the conservation status of the hen harrier.

The licence permits the removal of hen harrier eggs and/or chicks to a dedicated hatching and rearing facility, where they will be hand-reared in captivity, before being transferred to specially-constructed pens in hen harrier breeding habitat, from which they are then re-introduced into the wild in the uplands of northern England. This intervention may only occur where hen harrier nests have reached an agreed density.

Natural England experts have rigorously scrutinised the licence application and will work closely with the licence applicant throughout the duration of the trial to ensure that all elements are carried out proportionately and effectively, to bring about the best possible outcome for hen harriers.

Natural England Chairman, Andrew Sells, said:

"Improving the conservation status of hen harriers across England is something I feel very passionate about. The principles of this trial have been carefully researched by those best-placed to understand the conflict which can occur between hen harriers and driven grouse moors.

"It is a complicated and emotive picture and we have considered this application very carefully. Licensing this trial will allow important evidence to be gathered which, I sincerely hope, will lead to a self-sustaining and well-dispersed breeding population of these beautiful birds across England."

Amanda Anderson, Director of the Moorland Association said:

"The Moorland Association is delighted that Natural England has issued a ground-breaking research licence to test if brood management will help improve the Hen Harrier population and range in upland northern England. The Hen Harrier Brood Management Group has sought to provide a pragmatic solution to a proven predator-prey conflict while safeguarding important land use.

"Moorland managed for red grouse contributes significantly to remote rural communities, businesses and treasured landscapes. This new wildlife management licence will give land managers confidence that impacts of hen harriers breeding on their land can be minimised, creating a win-win scenario."

Dr Adam Smith of the Game & Wildlife Conservation Trust said:

"GWCT research has over many years described the tension between grouse moor management and hen harrier conservation. We believe it important that the hen harrier recovery plan includes this practical trial of a well understood raptor conservation tool, the brood management scheme. If successful, this approach should help hen harriers and red grouse thrive – in the interests of both, and of moorland."

16 January 2018

⇨   The above information is reprinted with kind permission from GOV.UK. Please visit www.gov.uk for further information.

© Crown copyright 2018

One of world's largest marine parks created off coast of Easter Island

Rapa Nui protection area, about the same size as the Chilean mainland, will protect up to 142 species, including 27 threatened with extinction.

By Arthur Neslen

One of the world's largest marine protection areas has been created off the coast of Easter Island.

The 740,000 sq km Rapa Nui marine park is roughly the size of the Chilean mainland and will protect at least 142 endemic marine species, including 27 threatened with extinction.

An astonishing 77% of the Pacific Ocean's fish abundance occurs here and recent expeditions discovered several new species previously unknown to science.

Apex predators found in the conservation zone include scalloped hammerhead sharks, minke, humpback and blue whales, and four species of sea turtle.

Matt Rand, the director of the Pew Bertarelli ocean legacy project, which campaigned for the park, said: "This marine reserve will have a huge global significance for the conservation of oceans and of indigenous people's ways of life.

"The Rapa Nui have long suffered from the loss of timber, declining eco-systems and declining populations. Now they are experiencing a resurgence based on ensuring the health of the oceans."

Plans for the marine park were first announced at a conference in 2015, at which the former US President Barack Obama declared his "special love for the ocean" in a video message.

The plans were confirmed in a speech by Chilean president Michelle Bachelet on Saturday.

The marine park's creation was enabled by a 73% vote in favour of the conservation zone from Easter Island's 3,000 Rapa Nui population in a referendum on 3 September, after five years of consultations.

Extractive industries and industrial fishing will be banned inside the reserve, but the Rapa Nui will be allowed to continue their traditional artisanal fishing on small boats, using hand lines with rocks for weights.

Ludovic Burns Tuki, the director of the Mesa del Mar coalition of more than 20 Rapa Nui groups, said: "This is a historic moment – a great and beautiful moment for the Rapa Nui, for the world and for our oceans.

"We think this process can be an example for the creation of other marine reserves that we need to protect our oceans – with a respect for the human dimension."

After the creation of a comparable marine protection area around the nearby Pitcairn Islands last year, proposals for a reserve in the Austral Islands' waters could soon create a protected area of more than 2 million sq km. This would have a unifying potential for the Polynesian people, according to Burns Tuki.

"The ocean is very important to us as a source of food, but the Polynesians were great navigators and the ocean also represents our mother," he said. "It enables us to move with a double canoe between the different islands.

It gives us everything."

As global warming takes hold, some scientific papers suggest that marine reserves may also help mitigate climate change and provide a vital carbon sink. The deep, clear and cool waters around Easter Island are also a resilient area for coral reefs.

Marcelo Mena, Chile's environment minister, said: "This marine protected area adds to the legacy of President Bachelet and the 1.5 million sq km of protected areas created by this government."

The International Union for Conservation of Nature has called for 30% of the world's oceans to be protected, but only about 1.6% has so far been covered by marine protection areas.

9 September 2017

⇨ The above information is reprinted with kind permission from *The Guardian*. Please visit www.theguardian.com for further information.

New tracking devices can help monitor the world's wildlife

A revolutionary new series of lightweight, long-lasting and low-cost wildlife tracking devices has been developed to enable scientists around the globe to monitor more wildlife.

The joint project between the University of East Anglia (UEA), the British Trust for Ornithology (BTO) and the Universities of Lisbon and Porto, was initiated because the need to follow animals is increasing as more adapt to a changing environment. By understanding their whole lifecycle, conservation strategies can be developed to help give them a more secure future.

The Movetech Telemetry devices are designed to collect detailed information about the behaviour of wildlife, which is transmitted to researchers using the mobile phone network. This means that, once fitted to an animal, there is no need to recapture it to retrieve the data. The addition of advanced solar cells makes it possible to track animals more efficiently in less sunny northern locations.

The new tags can be used on animals weighing as little as 600g, around the weight of a medium-sized gull, and will transmit vital data for up to 12 months, relaying details of exactly what the animal does and precisely where it is at any given time.

Dr Aldina Franco, a senior lecturer in Ecology at the School of Environmental Sciences, UEA, said: "With these devices we can track a large number of species, for example, white storks in Portugal or gull species here in the UK, but its applications reach far wider. We can study the movements of urban species and the impact of wind farms on birds' welfare and behaviour, as well as monitoring the success of conservation projects."

"The number of animal movement studies has grown exponentially in recent years, and an estimated 1,500 birds in the UK alone were fitted with tracking devices in 2015," said Dr Phil Atkinson from the British Trust for Ornithology. "The demand for smaller, lighter tracking devices is large and Movetech Telemetry devices will enable researchers and conservationists to gather more data and answer more questions than ever before."

Dr Joao Paulo Silva, from CIBIO-InBIO, University of Porto, and cE3c, Faculty of Sciences of the University of Lisbon, said: "These new devices provide accurate locations and accelerometer information, allowing scientists to identify the behaviour of the animals – even identifying, for example, when a bird is feeding. What's more, you can see all this happening while sitting in front of the computer!"

8 March 2017

⇨ The above information is reprinted with kind permission from The University of East Anglia. Please visit www.uea.ac.uk for further information.

© 2018 University of East Anglia

Huge public backing for councils to reduce grass-cutting to help save our bees

⇨ Reducing grass-cutting saves money for cash-strapped councils.

⇨ Nearly two-thirds (63%) of public say councils should be doing more to help protect our bees.

⇨ Buglife and Friends of the Earth launch council guide to help pollinators at Bee Summit, 6 April.

Over 80 per cent (81%) of the public back calls for councils to help Britain's under-threat bees by cutting areas of grass less often in parks and roadside verges to allow wild flowers to grow, a new YouGov poll for Friends of the Earth and Buglife reveals today.

The move would also be good news for cash-strapped local authorities, with councils already saving thousands of pounds every year by reducing grass-cutting.

The Friends of the Earth and Buglife YouGov survey also revealed:

⇨ almost two-thirds of the population (63%) agree that local councils should be doing more to protect Britain's bees

⇨ 88% support councils reducing the use of bee-harming pesticides

⇨ 92% support local authorities in planting more wildflowers and other bee-friendly plants in their local parks and community spaces.

Buglife and Friends of the Earth are urging councils to play their part in boosting the nation's bee populations with a new guide for local authorities on the measures they can take to help pollinators.

Helping Pollinators Locally – Developing a Local Pollinator Action Plan written by Friends of the Earth and Buglife is published today at a Bee Summit in central London. The summit is organised by Friends of the Earth and the Women's Institute.

Local councils urged to act on pollinators

Reducing grass cutting is a good way for cash-strapped councils to save money too. Burnley Borough Council, which is speaking at the Bee Summit, estimates that savings from meadow management (including reducing grass-cutting to benefit wildlife) are £58,000 p.a. – and are expected to increase. Dorset County Council also estimates that significant savings have been made from wildlife-friendly policies, such as allowing grass to grow.

Despite all the publicity about bee decline, only a handful of councils – including Dorset, Devon, Cornwall, East Sussex and Bristol – have introduced comprehensive pollinator action plans. Since 1900, the UK has lost 20 species of bee, and a further 35 are considered under threat of extinction. None are protected by law. Across Europe nearly one in ten wild bee species face extinction.

Helping Pollinators Locally – Developing a Local Pollinator Action Plan spells out some of the policies councils could undertake, including:

⇨ Use the planning system to protect and increase pollinator-friendly habitat.

⇨ Manage council-owned or council-managed land to benefit bees and other pollinators, including: cutting some areas of grass less often in parks and roadside verges to allow wild flowers to grow; reducing the use of bee-harming pesticides; planting more wildflowers and other bee-friendly plants in local parks and community spaces.

⇨ Encouraging others to act. Local authorities can work with and encourage schools, businesses, local communities and individuals to help develop the flower-rich environments which our native pollinators need. They can raise awareness of the work that is being done and why it matters. Bringing people and nature closer together benefits health and well-being.

Friends of the Earth chief executive Craig Bennett said:

"Local councils have a vital part to play in helping the UK's under-threat bee populations.

"Policies, such as allowing grass to grow on roadside verges and in certain areas in parks, will help bees, save cash-strapped councils money and are supported by the public too.

"We hope many more councils will stand up for our bees and nature and introduce comprehensive pollinator action plans in the months ahead."

Dr Paul Evans, Lead Pollinator Advisor at Buglife said:

"We are not advocating abandoning areas of council land but introducing a new less-intensive form of grassland management. Effectively cutting grass less in the right places will not only help to counter pollinator decline it will benefit wildlife and people too. The message is a win, win, win for councils save money, help nature, enrich people's lives."

Simon Goff Head of Green Spaces & Amenities at Burnley Council, and who is speaking at today's Bee Summit said:

"People visit parks to enjoy contact with nature and so we are adopting a more ecological approach to managing them, with large areas of previously mown grass now managed as meadows. This saves money, reduces CO2 emissions, increases biodiversity and creates more attractive and interesting parks.

"The Council is facing huge cuts and so we are rethinking how we manage our greenspaces. We are focussing on what is important to park users such as removing litter, maintaining play areas and tackling dog fouling and we are saving money in other areas such as introducing more meadow areas and replacing expensive bedding schemes with herbaceous perennials."

Peter Moore, Environment Service Director at Dorset County Council, which has introduced a pollinator action plan that includes less grass-cutting, and who is speaking at the Bee Summit said:

"Dorset County Council adopted a new strategy for managing highway verges in 2014. We have a more targeted approach to the cutting we do, and we have introduced wildlife-friendly techniques. We estimate this has saved us £100,000 over the last two years, with a further £50,000 in savings anticipated in 2017–18. A significant amount of this saving is due to reducing the frequency of cutting, showing that pollinator-friendly approaches can save money too."

Marylyn Haines Evans, Public Affairs Chair of the NFWI commented:

"WI members have worked tirelessly to highlight the plight of honeybees by creating bee havens in back gardens, parks and on disused land. We know habitat loss is a key factor behind the decline of honeybees and other pollinators, so it is really positive to see local authorities take up the challenge to support pollinators in their own local communities.

"It is vital that we all play our part to support our precious honeybees, and we hope the guide will prompt more local authorities to work together with their local community to help pollinators thrive."

4 April 2017

⇨   The above information is reprinted with kind permission from Buglife. Please visit www.buglife.org.uk for further information.

Make these lifestyle changes and help secure the Galapagos' future

By Liz Bonnin, Science and natural history presenter and Terrific Scientific ambassador

Getting the chance to visit Galapagos last year was a dream come true for me. For years I had watched documentaries and read books about these enchanted islands and as a biologist I dearly wanted to witness the dramatic volcanic landscapes, harbouring the most extraordinary myriad of species.

Thanks in no small part to the legacy of Charles Darwin's groundbreaking journey on *HMS Beagle*, and the unique ecology of these islands, Galapagos is never out of the conservation spotlight. This has resulted in the protection of 97% of the archipelago, and the opportunity for a unique wildlife experience. It's one of the last places on Earth where you can experience wildlife as it might have looked before our human footprint began to make its presence felt.

Here, it's possible to wander amongst basking marine iguanas, sea lion pups learning to survive as they mimic their mothers, male fur seals jostling for supremacy, with majestic Galapagos hawks presiding over the scene. No animal pays the slightest bit of attention to you, and it feels like you are part of nature, not merely a spectator of it. Such a wildlife encounter leaves a powerful impression – this is a place where you can breathe, wonder at the beauty of our planet, and even perhaps renew your faith that in some places at least we are getting things right.

But Galapagos is not immune to the impact of the modern world. It is bowing under the pressure of our human footprint like never before – under the tonnes of plastics deposited on its shores every year, as a result of

the dramatic reduction of endemic species because of the invasive species we've introduced, and as it mourns the loss of all but one of its coral reefs as the oceans continue to warm.

And yet somehow, despite the countless documentaries showcasing this extraordinary, other-worldly place, despite the thousands of visitors who are lucky enough to lose themselves here for a while, there remains a disconnect about our relationship with this magnificent place. Somehow we still think that this is someone else's problem to fix.

But here's the thing. Galapagos matters. It matter to us, here in the UK. The island chain's ecosystem is inextricably connected to all other ecosystems on the planet, which means that what we do here at home affects Galapagos, and all the other precious wild places left on Earth for that matter. If we allow the health of Galapagos to falter, our own health will inevitable fail.

It can be a difficult concept to grasp, and we humans are superbly good at short-term vision and even sticking our heads in the sand, especially when there is so much going on in the world that seems to demand our attention. But there are many small and easy changes we can decide to make to our lives today that can make a very real difference. And next time we marvel at the beauty of places like Galapagos we can proudly know that daily, we are helping to secure their future:

⇨   Decide today that you will never use a straw again. Refuse them in bars and fast food restaurants. In

the UK alone, just from McDonald's outlets, 35 million straws are discarded every day and they are one of the biggest culprits when it comes to the destruction of our marine wildlife.

⇨ Buy a reusable coffee cup and never throw away another unrecyclable cup from the plethora of coffee shops that still refuse to provide eco-friendly ones.

⇨ Do the same with your water bottle. And rest easy that you are not ingesting leached chemicals from single use plastic bottles.

⇨ Book your next holiday to a sustainable eco-lodge that contributes to local communities, become a member of citizen science and volunteer to monitor wildlife there and contribute to the protection of ecosystems. It will be the most rewarding and feel-good holiday you'll ever go on.

⇨ Meat lovers have the highest carbon footprint. Cut down on red meat and do your bit to reduce greenhouse gas emissions from livestock farming, which produces up to 50% of all man-made emissions.

⇨ Change your light bulbs to compact fluorescent bulbs. They last for years and save you money – it's a no brainer.

⇨ Refrigerators are the biggest consumers of electricity in the home. Even turning down your thermostat by one degree makes a big difference. In the winter turn it down by two degrees.

⇨ Turn off the water when you are brushing your teeth. This is an easy habit to develop and saving every bit of water adds up.

⇨ Eat less and eat more organic, local produce to reduce the use of toxic chemicals in the environment and the carbon

footprint from transport vehicles. We all eat too much anyway, and the more we demand organic food as consumers the lower the prices will get.

⇨ Speak up and make your voice heard to your local government representative. It's time to proudly take ownership of protecting the wild places we love. Spread the word and tell your friends. It feels really good, even empowering, to make these changes together.

16 July 2017

⇨ The above information is reprinted with kind permission from The Huffington Post UK. Please visit www.huffingtonpost.co.uk for further information.

Key facts

⇨ Over 750,000 square kilometres of Amazon rainforest have been cleared since 1970 – a fifth of the total. (page 1)

⇨ Wildlife is dying out due to habitat destruction, over hunting, toxic pollution, invasion by alien species and climate change. (page 2)

⇨ 2014 analysis of 3,000 species indicated that 50% of individual animals have been lost since 1970. (page 3)

⇨ The growing human population – which has increased by 130 per cent in the last 50 years and is set to rise to more than ten billion by 2060. (page 4)

⇨ Earth is capable of providing healthy diets for ten billion people in 2060 and preserving viable habitats for the vast majority of its remaining species. (page 4)

⇨ Migratory birds are arriving earlier and egg-laying dates have advanced such that swallows, are arriving in the UK 15 days earlier, and breeding 11 days earlier, than they did in the 1960s. (page 5)

⇨ 90% of the world's fisheries are already fully exploited or overfished. (page 6)

⇨ They might cover over 70% of our planet's surface, but only a tiny fraction of the oceans has been protected: just 3.4%. (page 6)

⇨ Western black rhinoceros, once roamed sub-Saharan Africa, but fell victim to poaching. Its population was in the hundreds in 1980, fell to ten by 2000, and just five a year later. Surveys in 2006 failed to locate any and it was declared extinct in 2011. (page 7)

⇨ The Steller's sea cow reached up to nine metres in length but was hunted to extinction in 1768, within 27 years of its discovery by Europeans. (page 8)

⇨ Turtle doves are on the brink of extinction in the UK because of farming practices. (page 10)

⇨ Latest statistics from the Environment Department (Defra) revealed that birds living and breeding on the UK's farmland saw numbers tumble by almost a tenth between 2010 and 2015. (page 10)

⇨ Trophy hunting is an important industry – a greater land area of sub-Saharan Africa is conserved for hunting than is protected in national parks. (page 12)

⇨ It is estimated that there could be as many as 14 million species of plants and animals in the world, although only around two million have been officially recorded so far. More than 12,000 species of animals and plants now face extinction, due largely to human activities. Some will die out before they have even been discovered. (page 14)

⇨ Tropical rainforests are the world's richest natural habitats, housing more than two-thirds of all plant and animal species on Earth. (page 14)

⇨ Six species of great ape who live in the tropical rainforests – the eastern and western gorilla, chimpanzee, bonobo, Sumatran and Bornean orang-utan – now face extinction. (page 14)

⇨ At the beginning of the 20th century, there were more than 100,000 tigers. Today, it is estimated that between 5,000 and 7,000 tigers remain in the wild. (page 14)

⇨ Rhinos have roamed the Earth for more than 40 million years, but after only a few centuries of intensive hunting they are now severely threatened. The world population of all five species is fewer than 15,000 animals. (page 14)

⇨ Researchers are sounding the alarm for the helmeted hornbill after a new study revealed 2,170 hornbill heads or casques had been confiscated from illegal trade in just three years. (page 18)

⇨ In 2015, due to the severe increase in poaching for the illegal trade, the helmeted hornbill was reclassified from Near Threatened to Critically Endangered on the IUCN Red List of Threatened Species. (page 18)

⇨ The black rhino population is estimated to be just over 5,000 individuals; the greater one-horn rhino over 3,500, and the Javan and Sumatran rhinos both under 100. (page 19)

⇨ An Irish organised crime group, the Rathkeale Rovers, is allegedly responsible for 60 rhino horn thefts from natural history museums across Europe. (page 19)

⇨ 47 per cent of terrestrial [non-flying] threatened mammals (out of 873 species) and 23.4 per cent of threatened birds (out of 1,272 species) may have already been negatively impacted by climate change in at least part of their distribution. (page 20)

⇨ Only about 450 North Atlantic right whales exist, and only 100 of them are breeding females. 17 of the animals washed up dead in 2017. (page 23)

⇨ Giraffe populations have declined by 40 per cent in the last 30 years, and there are now thought to be fewer than 98,000 individuals remaining in the wild. (page 25)

⇨ The plight of Africa's lions is lamentable. Since the 1960s, the world has lost at least 70% of these magnificent cats. (page 29)

⇨ The natural life expectancy of a lion living in the wild rarely exceeds 13 years. (page 29)

⇨ The International Union for Conservation of Nature has called for 30% of the world's oceans to be protected, but only about 1.6% has so far been covered by marine protection areas. (page 35)

⇨ Since 1900, the UK has lost 20 species of bee, and a further 35 are considered under threat of extinction. (page 37)

Conservation
Safeguarding biodiversity; attempting to protect endangered species and their habitats from destruction.

Deforestation
The clearance of large areas of forest to obtain wood or land for cattle grazing.

Ecosystem
A system maintained by the interaction between different biological organisms within their physical environment, each one of which is important for the ecosystem to continue to function efficiently.

Endangered species
An animal which is at risk of becoming extinct.

Environment
The complex set of physical, geographic, biological, social, cultural and political conditions that surround an individual or organism and that ultimately determine its form and the nature of its survival.

Evolution
A gradual change in animals or plants over generations, during which they change their physical characteristics.

Extinct
If a species has become extinct, there are no surviving members of that species: it has died out completely.

Habitat
An area which supports certain conditions, allowing various species native to that area to live and thrive. When a species' "natural habitat" is mentioned, this refers to the area it would usually occupy in the wild.

Hunting
Hunting is the killing or animals for food or sport. Includes trophy hunting, where people kill animals and keep and display their body parts.

IUCN Red List of Threatened Species
The most commonly-used measure of how endangered a species has become is the IUCN Red List, which classifies endangered species as either Critically Endangered (CR), meaning that a species faces extremely high risk of extinction in the near future; Endangered (EN), meaning that a species faces a very high risk of extinction in the near future and Vulnerable (VU), meaning that a species is likely to become Endangered unless the circumstances threatening its survival and reproduction improve.

Natural extinction
If a species becomes extinct due to natural causes (as opposed to human causes such as poaching).

Poaching
Similar to hunting, but the animals are killed without permission or illegally.

Rewilding
Reintroducing a species that previously inhabited a natural area.

Species
A specific type of living organism.

Threatened species
An animal which is at risk of becoming an endangered species unless the circumstances threatening its extinction change.

Wildlife
A collective term for wild animals and plants that grow and live independently of human beings.

Wildlife trade
The sale of wild animals, increasingly achieved through use of the Internet to advertise and promote auctions.

Assignments

Brainstorming

⇨ Brainstorm what you know about extinction:

- What are some of the causes of extinction?

- Which species do you think are most at risk?

- List as many species you can think of that are already extinct.

Research

⇨ Do some research into the types of insects which are at risk of extinction. What is causing the decline in their numbers? Write some notes on your findings and share with the rest of your class.

⇨ Conduct a questionnaire amongst your year group to find out what they know about species in decline. Ask at least six questions and write a short report on your findings.

⇨ Research how warming seas are affecting different species of birds and the prey they feed on. Make some notes and tell your class what you found out.

⇨ In pairs, do some research into whether trophy hunting might help in the conservation of lions. Look into how the population of large animals in Kenya, Tanzania and Zambia declined after hunting was banned in 1977. You should consider the African population who lose crops, livestock and even their lives to species such as the lion. Write a short report which should cover at least one A4 side and share with the rest of your class.

⇨ Do some research into tracking devices. What animals can they be used on and what do they tell us about their movements and behaviour. Make some notes and feedback to your class.

Design

⇨ In small groups create a leaflet to inform people about extinction. Choose a particular species in Africa and explain why it is important to preserve it.

⇨ Choose one of the articles in this book and create an illustration to highlight its key themes.

⇨ Design a leaflet highlighting the threat to bumblebees. You should consider the impact their decline would have on plant life.

⇨ Imagine you are working for a wildlife group who are working to protect the cheetah. Create a poster which could be displayed in public places that will highlight your cause.

⇨ In groups, design plans for a marine park. You should consider where this park will be, what area it would cover and what wildlife and plants it will help preserve.

Oral

⇨ As a class, discuss how you think climate change is threatening many species in the ocean and what you think could be done to change this.

⇨ Choose one of the illustrations for this book and, in pairs, discuss what you think the artist was trying to portray with their image. Would you change the illustration in any way?

⇨ In small groups, prepare a PowerPoint presentation that shows the species most at risk of extinction and why. Share your findings with your class.

⇨ As a class look at the article on page 4 and discuss the statement: "The world is currently facing its sixth mass extinction". Discuss the causes and what action we could take to hep prevent this from happening.

⇨ As a class, stage a debate around the question: "Should trophy hunting be allowed?" Half the class should argue 'for' and half 'against'.

Reading/writing

⇨ Write a one-paragraph definition of 'Extinction' and then compare it with a classmates.

⇨ Watch the film *Racing Extinction* by Louie Psihoyos and write a review exploring the issues raised by this film.

⇨ Read the article on page 37, 'Huge public backing for councils to reduce grass-cutting to help save our bees'. Write a letter to your local council asking them if they are prepared to reduce their grass-cutting and explaining the reasons why this is important. You should also ask them to consider reducing the amount of bee-harming pesticides they use. Ask them if they would consider planting more wild flowers in their local parks and community areas.

⇨ Write an article explaining the reasons farming practices are causing the near extinction of turtle doves. Explain why you think it is important that we prevent their further decline.

⇨ Read the article on page 30, 'Inside the frozen zoo where eggs and sperm are stored to help endangered animals and write a summary for your school newspaper.

Acknowledgements

The publisher is grateful for permission to reproduce the material in this book. While every care has been taken to trace and acknowledge copyright, the publisher tenders its apology for any accidental infringement or where copyright has proved untraceable. The publisher would be pleased to come to a suitable arrangement in any such case with the rightful owner.

Images

All images courtesy of iStock except pages 1, 5, 6, 10, 12, 23, 24, 26 and 35: Pixabay, pages 6, 19, 21, 22: Morguefile, pages 32 and 33 Unsplash

Illustrations

Don Hatcher: pages 15 & 22. Simon Kneebone: pages 13 & 36. Angelo Madrid: pages 16 & 39.

Additional acknowledgements

With thanks to the Independence team: Shelley Baldry, Danielle Lobban, Jackie Staines and Jan Sunderland.

Tina Brand

Cambridge, June 2018